THE NATURALIST IN WALES

THE NATURALIST IN

Wales

R. M. LOCKLEY

DAVID & CHARLES : NEWTON ABBOT

Set in 12 on 13 point Bembo
and printed in Great Britain
by Latimer Trend & Company Limited
for David & Charles (Publishers) Limited
South Devon House Newton Abbot Devon

Contents

List of Illustrations

Preface

THIS BOOK IS intended to help the naturalist visiting or living in Wales who, like myself, has a general interest in the countryside, and in particular to guide the amateur in search of birds and flowers. I have lived all my life in Wales, yet have not found a single book which covers nature in Wales adequately. Nor indeed can one slender volume be more than an introduction to the vast subject. The nearest perhaps has been a book I treasured in my youth, George Bolam's *Wild Life in Wales*, published in 1913, but written still earlier: entertaining, discursive, and now almost an historical document on the distribution of species early in this century. That distribution has altered vastly—not always alas for the better—some species have become rarer, but others have been more precisely located, and discovered or re-discovered in new sites. Specialists have begun to study the ecology (including the distribution) of many species of mammals, birds, plants, insects and fishes, amphibia and reptiles in Wales.

To the naturalist Wales is a remarkable and beautiful country, a separate peninsular kingdom of nature forming an ecological entity in her own right. It was George Borrow who wrote in 1851 that there is nothing like the scenery of Wales in all the world: grander there may be, he thought, and scenery more soft and lovely, but none in which grandeur and loveliness meet and mingle in so fascinating a way. And as for the kind-hearted Welsh people he met, Borrow believed that no other race was so poetic, so romantic and—because of their resistance to oppression by the Saxon—'so noble yet pathetic'. All this is shrewd if sentimental comment, by a remarkably perceptive observer who taught himself Welsh and translated the Welsh poets before

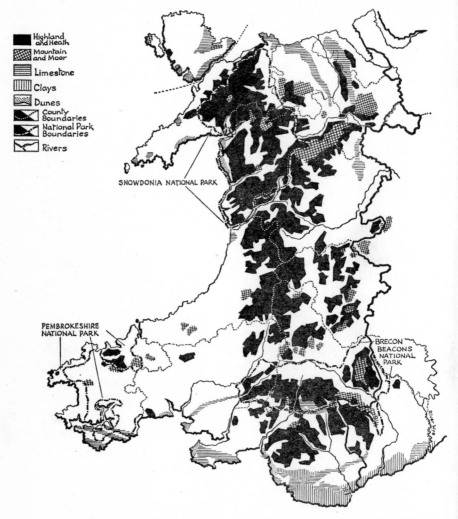

Figure 1   The shape of Wales: principal geological and physical features, and political boundaries

ever coming to Wales; and who gives his readers the sensible warning that to see Wales in all her loveliness, and to meet her people, it is necessary to go on foot. We echo this: the roads were narrow then, and although some of them are better sur-faced now, they are still delightfully winding and narrow; the wise naturalist will leave his car behind and make his most suc-cessful explorations afoot into the roadless mountain and deep *cwm* by the ancient paths and trackways. There he will find still a people pathetic only in the noble sense of unworldliness, cour-tesy, and inability to wish to outwit 'the sly Saxon'—as Borrow contemptuously labelled the English trader.

Physically Wales is quite distinct from England, separated from the smooth rich lowlands (the Marches) by her massif of low mountains. Two main rivers running through dense swamp and oak forest defined the isthmus of old: the Severn in the south, the Dee in the north. The headwaters of these rivers lie close together in the Welsh mountains, those beautiful barriers which long made Wales a fastness not easily penetrated by her enemies.

Culturally these mountains of the west are the last retreat of the Celtic peoples who formerly occupied all Britain before the invasions of the Romans, who knew them as the British. When the Saxons arrived following the departure of the Roman legions, they too failed to advance far into Wales, although they conquered England. They were fiercely resisted after crossing the plains of Severn and Dee, the Welsh (British) making deadly counter-attacks and wiping out all settlements west of the rivers. So much so that about AD 784 the Saxon leader Offa of Mercia constructed a broad tall earthen dyke to contain the Welsh. The line of Offa's Dyke is still plain, and may be walked today along much of its length, as it follows very nearly the present boun-daries of Wales from Prestatyn in Flint, south through Mont-gomery and Radnor shires as far as the deep ravine and turbulent water of the upper Wye river.

In this book we are concerned only with the present limits of this peninsula of Wales, as contained within her twelve counties,

plus the southern border county of Monmouth. The last is sometimes claimed politically by England, but physically it is a natural
part of Wales, clearly separated from England by the river Wye
and containing part of the higher Welsh mountains. While its
preponderance of truly Welsh place-names clearly shows where
this county's ethnic roots belong.

We have only to glance at the physical map of Wales (figure I,
page IO) to see how conveniently this peninsular territory is
defined by the sea on three sides, and by mountain escarpment,
Offa's Dyke and flowing river on the fourth, the inner or isthmus
side. Within these limits Wales is satisfyingly aloof topographi-
cally, as well as ethnologically and climatically; as we shall see
when exploring a land of sequestered mountains, rolling moors
and deep remote valleys, a land which to the naturalist promises
days of specific discovery amid unspoilt, beautiful and often
dramatic scenery.

CHAPTER ONE

The Shape of Wales

Geography and geology — Climate — Rainfall

THE SHAPE OF Wales, her geography and geology, was born out of earth, and fathered by weather. The vivid scenery, the apparently changeless rocks, however much and long these have been praised by poets, and sometimes condemned by travellers, are none the less impermanent in terms of geological time. They have been altered by constant attrition, denudation and disintegration, addition and replacement by new layers of sediment, violent volcanic upheaval, and by rearrangement through buckling and folding of the earth's crust. The student of geology discovers that here is a subject which reflects the complicated and fascinating history of earth, which is full of exciting change and flux. There is eternity in a grain of sand only because its molecules and atoms never disappear, but merely transmute, form new combinations, build new particles, changing their chemistry as water and earth pressures lift them up, or bear them down, solidifying into rock, blowing away on the wind.

The characteristic rocks of Wales can be shown in the form of a simplified history of the laying down, or stratification, as in figure 2 of the high tops and uplands of Snowdonia and Cader Idris. Their craggy beauty is due to the outpouring of magma (molten rock) from early volcanoes, the resultant solidified lava of which is more resistant to weather than the less competent sedimentary rocks which it covers or by which it may have been covered in subsequent sinking of the land below the sea. When earth movements cause a new period of mountain building the

13

layers of volcanic and sedimentary rocks may be forced upwards
and cracked open to our view in surface outcrops at any angle
between horizontal and vertical. These rocks—their petrology
and fossils (if any)—enable the geologist to reconstruct the broad
outlines of the history of the living land, by careful mapping and
detailed comparison.

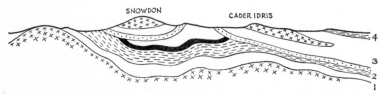

Figure 2   Simplified diagram of rock strata, Snowdonia National Park, at the
present day. The geological systems are numbered: 1, oldest, Pre-
Cambrian; 2, Cambrian; 3, Ordovician; 4, Silurian. Above 4 once
lay the Devonian (Old Red Sandstone), and above the Devonian
once lay the Cretaceous (Chalk); both these have been denuded,
although present in other parts of Wales (see figure 4), and with the
effects of folding and volcanic action the harder igneous rock now
crowns the summits of Snowdon and Cader Idris

It is a fascinating jigsaw, but commonly many pieces are missing. When this happens it is almost certain that the lost layers of
rock from the recognised sequence of bedding planes has been
denuded, worn away by rain, water or wind over a long period
before a later layer of sediment has been laid down. The omission
is known geologically as an unconformity.

Figure 2 shows that the major volcanic activity occurred in
the Ordovician period of Ancient Life (Palaeozoic) Era, 435–500
million years ago, when a chain of volcanic pipes thrust the
igneous rock to the surface to form part of the heights, notably
of Snowdon and Cader Idris, and some lower mountains south
to Mynydd Preselau in Pembrokeshire. Some of this Ordovician
volcanic material was extruded on land and some under the sea.

Because the rock exposures in Wales were often vivid in her
scenery they were studied early in the history of geological research. Consequently some of the classified periods were given

names, which are now in worldwide use, from the districts in which they were first studied: Cambrian and Pre-Cambrian for all the earliest rocks, taken from the Latin name for Wales; Ordovician and Silurian, from the ancient British tribes of the Ordovices and Silures inhabiting Wales and her borders.

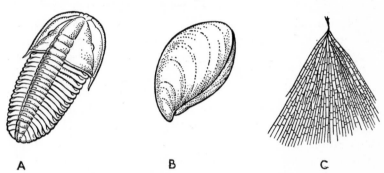

A   B   C

Figure 3   Fossils from Cambrian rocks: A, Trilobite; B, Brachiopod; C, Graptolite

The earliest fossils in Wales are found in the Cambrian rocks. Such are the louse-like tribolites; the stationary brachiopods with a two-valved shell resembling a modern cockle and persisting today in very little altered descendant species; and the floating far-wandering graptolites (figure 3). Evolving swiftly—in terms of geological time—into new forms, these fossils, with corals, lived on for millions of years into Ordovician centuries. By so doing they have enabled geologists to divide the Ordovician rock system into five series of strata, or group of layers, according to the contained species of fossil. In Wales the arrangement is (youngest on top):

    5 Caradoc series
    4 Ashgill series (5 and 4 together form the Bala series)
    3 Llandeilo series
    2 Llanvirn series
    1 Arenig series

This was the main period of volcanic activity, and each volcano can be roughly dated from the species of fossils buried in the sediments adjacent to its lava flows. Volcanic activity in Wales lasted probably 25 million years, to be followed by the Silurian epoch of 35–45 million years which was devoted partly to mountain building, as it merged into the Devonian period. This was a time of very widespread earth movement, folding and uplift, known as the Caledonian Earth Movement (figure 2).

Silurian and Devonian deposits are thickest in South Wales, but quite shallow or missing in much of the Snowdon region, washed away as the land rose above sea-level. Pressures converted muddy shales into slates.

The land of Wales was to sink several times again during the long Carboniferous period of 60 million years, and again 70 million years later in the Cretaceous or Chalk period. Beds of the Carboniferous Limestone are widely exposed in South Wales (figure 4), less so in the north; but all the chalk layers in Wales have been washed away. They were too near the surface, too soft, and were denuded when the last (Cainozoic) mountain building period, which shaped the present land of Wales, set in some 50 million years ago.

Southwards and eastwards of the weather-washed heights of Snowdonia—also in Anglesey—the younger layers of the Devonian Old Red Sandstone and the still younger limestone have survived in large tracts at the surface, giving rich colour to the ploughlands of the border counties with red sandy soils and blue-white cliffs. This limestone produces excellent rock for grinding into cement because it contains few impurities.

Above the limestone are the shales and sandstones laid down as the land ceased to sink, and began to rise, producing vast swampy regions where rooted the ferns and trees of the coal seams. Subsequently much of this one-time forest area was denuded again, before the sediments had solidified under pressure to coal. The extensive Coal Measures of South Wales are much folded and squeezed between the Pennant Sandstone above and the Millstone Grit below. Miners call the upper part of the millstone grit 'Farewell Rock': it was useless to drill for coal below it. Figure 4 shows in simplified form the geology of the

Page 17 *(left)* 'The Green Bridge of Wales', a limestone arch on the south Pembrokeshire coast; *(right)* Llyn Padarn, looking into Llanberis Pass, Snowdonia

Page 18 (above) The Brecon Beacons from Craig Cerrig Gleisiad Nature Reserve; (below) Skokholm Island faces north-west at the edge of 3,000 miles of open Atlantic, and is the nesting island of 35,000 Manx shearwaters, 2,000 storm petrels and other sea birds, with many rare birds recorded on migration

B

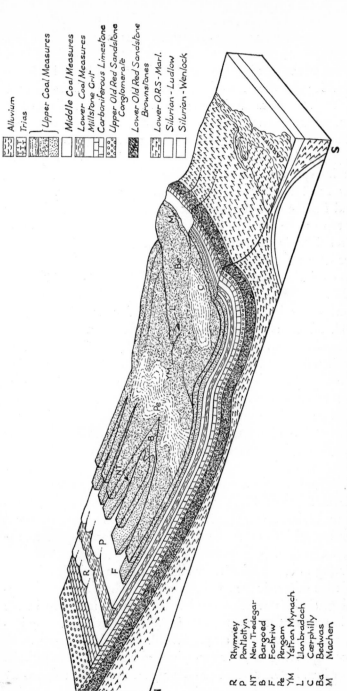

Figure 4　Simplified block diagram of the South Wales geology (N – S = 30 miles)

Alluvium
Trias
Upper Coal Measures
Middle Coal Measures
Lower Coal Measures
Millstone Grit
Carboniferous Limestone
Upper Old Red Sandstone Conglomerate
Lower Old Red Sandstone Brownstones
Lower O.R.S.-Marl.
Silurian - Ludlow
Silurian - Wenlock

R   Rhymney
P   Pontlottyn
NT   New Tredegar
B   Bargoed
F   Fochriw
Pe   Pengam
YM   Ystran Mynach
L   Llanbradach
C   Caerphilly
Ba   Bedwas
M   Machen

younger rocks just mentioned, which predominate in South
Wales. See also the map of the Brecon Beacons National Park
(page 174). So we reach the end, the topmost layers, of rock laid
down, before the next period, the Glacial or Pleistocene or Ice
Age, began the smoothing and polishing of the surface of Wales
during the last million years and less. Finally our present
Atlantic-type weather has put the finishing touches to the
features and drainage of the land as we know it today.

Had I more space I should like to have described the many
rock types to be found in Wales, and to discuss their distribution
and relationship to scenery in Wales as a whole. I cannot do
better than refer the more serious student to the splendid col-
lection of these types in the National Museum of Wales at
Cardiff.

During the hundreds of thousands of years of the glacial
period, the climate of northern Europe at intervals became as
cold as Greenland is today. Summers were insufficiently warm
to melt winter snows, which compacted into ice on the high
ground. The shallow Irish Sea froze solid, and the waters of the
ocean shrank from the land as rivers ceased to flow into the sea.
Instead glacier ice up to 1,000 ft thick began to flow from the
heights of Snowdon, meeting the ice grinding its way south over
the shallow dried-out sea. The sea-ice carried marine gravel and
shells up from the bed of the Irish Sea, to be deposited many
miles inland, even on mountain slopes 1,000 ft above present
sea-level. Some of the glacial ice travelled far south, from Scotland to Wales, carrying with it huge boulders, clay, slate and
other material from the northern source right down to the
Bristol Channel.

During intervals of warmer climate the ice melted, releasing
its burden of erratic rock and foreign soil. There are four recognised glaciations which have left their mark indelibly in the
development of ice-cut features in Wales: particularly the ice-
cut mountain corrie or cirque (Welsh equivalent—*cwm*), with
its accompanying arete or razor-backed ridge (*crib*), and glacial
lake or *llyn*, in Snowdonia and the higher mountain chain as far

south as the Brecon Beacons. The characteristic mountain lake or llyn was formed at the melting of the glaciers which deposited their load of rock and soil in a terminal moraine or dam, which held the old meltwater and the new living rain. The deepest of these is Llyn Cowlyd, 222 ft, in Snowdonia; perhaps because it has no substantial streams feeding it with silt. In South Wales the largest natural lake is much shallower: Llangorse (Llyn Syfaddan) is nowhere deeper than 28 ft, scooped out of a rock basin by the ancient glacial ice, and now slowly filling up with silt from streams and the river Llynfi.

The last Ice Age was limited in Wales: the ice reached as far south as north Pembrokeshire, where it dammed the north-flowing rivers so that they became lakes and rose high enough to flow south into the ice-free Bristol Channel, which was at that time, due to the shrinking of the sea, a river valley. Here roamed the hardy Ice-Age animals such as hairy mammoth, reindeer, musk ox, cave bear, wolf and other beasts hunted by Neanderthal man. Ireland was then joined to Scotland, perhaps also to Wales; and England was not separated from Europe.

In our present moment of time the land of Wales survives in what is possibly an interval between the last Ice Age (about 10,000 years ago) and the next, enjoying a suboceanic climate, said to be getting milder and wetter. The sea is still slowly rising around most of the coast of Wales, even though blown sand adds new land to some shores; or else the land is sinking under earth movements. The fiord of Milford Haven is said to be sinking at the rate of about 1 mm each year; as a result of this drowning, the valley provides one of the world's deepest harbours, accommodating the giant tankers which dock at Milford's several new 'ocean terminal' piers.

In hitherto puny fashion man has done much scratching and little altering of the land; but increasingly of late huge power-driven machines eat their way in search of rock and ore for commercial profit, or tear strips of motorway through the countryside. Where it will lead, this development of huge earth and rock-moving machinery, is a dream of the engineers, not of the naturalists, who prefer to save the countryside from further development, and are content to note the sequel to man's earlier efforts to shift the rock to his purpose. In small, now disused, quarries all over Wales, since the building of stone houses and tombs began much more than 2,000 years ago, you may see that evidence, now pleasingly softened and enriched by time, weather and interesting plant life on the steep faces, which are secure from the attacks of grazing mammals. These old scars provide variety within the more sophisticated smooth areas of long-settled country, and are miniature nature reserves for species driven from cultivated fields and bulldozed hedges. Many occur on steep uncultivable escarpments, often now clothed in trees and bushes, where few people visit, and badgers and foxes make their homes in the soil and disintegrated shale at the base of the rock.

In the slate-yielding districts of North Wales, and in the coal-fields of South Wales and the borders, huge tips of rock and spoil disfigure the landscape. The naturalist turns from them in disgust. Yet it is interesting to see that some tips, unused for thirty years or longer, have greened over, and even become covered with trees. And it is a policy of the nationalised coal industry today to plant these old tips, or lease or sell them to forestry interests, now that it is known that conifers and other commercially viable trees will grow in the disintegrating spoil.

Excavation of limestone rock for cement and land lime production has not infrequently opened out very old cave systems, some of which have contained the bones of the Neanderthal period, mentioned above. Where rivers still run through limestone valleys, as in the upper Neath and Tawe watershed (just inside the Brecon Beacons Park) there is the most enchanting scenery of waterfalls, pot-holes, caves and cliffs, rich with lime-loving flora. The river frequently disappears underground in fine dry weather, entering long caverns which are explored by keen speceologists. Members of caving clubs never tire of ranging the labyrinth underground, and of late some exciting new passages and galleries of considerable length and size have been discovered in South Wales (pages 173, 183).

Mention must also be made of the canals, few in Wales and largely an extension from English river systems. They are no longer used for heavy freight, carried today at speed by road. Some have become blocked from long disuse, with stretches filled in. Most of the old towpaths are delightful sauntering grounds for the naturalist, who can study the rich aquatic life of weedy but clean, undisturbed water under overhanging alders and willows. The longest all-Welsh canal, which runs between Brecon and Newport, has now been cleaned out sufficiently to be used for small pleasure craft; it passes through the beautiful valley of the Usk, between the Brecon Beacons and the Black Mountains, and must be the most scenically attractive navigable waterway in all England and Wales (see pages 178-9).

Climate

As part of the European land mass before the enislement of Britain the land of Wales experienced a gradual warming of climate as the ice of the last glacial period melted over 10,000 years ago. We can infer that the ground at the foot of the retreating ice became covered with grass during subsequent summers, but was treeless. It was an arctic climate with park-like tundra, but farther south, on the lower ground, taiga (birch forest) would grow. Here roamed the hairy mammoth whose enormously long tusks, curving round inwards at their extremities, were an efficient instrument for sweeping the snow aside and scraping the thick moss into position for the trunk to convey it to the mouth. There was also a woolly rhinoceros adapted to cool arctic conditions; but it is uncertain if these huge beasts had acquired a fur coat because they had been forced to do so by the advancing ice earlier, or because, in competition for food with the naked elephants and rhinoceroses of more tropical southern regions, they had been driven north to the ice limit. From time to time, one of these hairy giants would fall into bog or ice crevasse, and become preserved. The Siberian tundra was a last refuge; mammoth flesh, thousands of years old, has been found so well preserved here, that when properly cooked it has even been eaten by man.

There are no written references to our climate farther back than Roman times, when already the weather of Wales was described as wet and windy by visiting historians. But fortunately the deposits of peat are a rough-and-ready book of the history of the climate in the region of their laying down. With the use of a long boring cylinder to extract a core of peat, the expert can examine its original order of deposition from base soil upwards to the surface. Such a core may be more than ten feet long to reach the bottom of the peat bog. Samples are then taken every two or three inches along the core, and each sample is treated with dilute nitric acid. This destroys the humus, but hardens the undecayed plant remains. In particular, as pollen is the most resistant part of a plant, the pollen produced by forest trees each year during the growth of the peat bog is laid down and preserved in successive layers. By carefully counting the distinctive grains of pollen of tree species in each sample layer, it is possible to discover which tree was dominant at the time the layer of peat was laid down.

As a result of the construction of a great number of such pollen diagrams from Welsh and English bogs the general sequence of forest types and their related climates has been ascertained, as far back as the late glacial period where the bog dates from that age.

Table 1 shows that for about 5,000 years following the last glaciation the land dried out under the warming climate. It has since become cooler and wetter, with alder pollen dominating over the last 5,000 years.

It was in this warmer period, 6000 to 0 years BC, that man came back to inhabit Wales in its present shape, permanently. The Romans arrived towards the end of the warm dry period, and moved out at the beginning of the present cool Atlantic phase. Except for slightly wetter or drier centuries the climate of

Wales has not changed much in the present Christian era of nearly 2,000 years.

Forest type	Climate	Period	Time
Alder–Birch Oak–Beech	Cold and wet	Sub-Atlantic	2000 AD – 0
Alder-mixed Oak Forest (with more Hazel)	Warm and dry	Sub-Boreal	2000 BC –
Alder-mixed Oak Forest	Warm and wet	Atlantic	4000 BC –
Hazel–Pine Hazel–Birch–Pine	Warm and dry	Boreal	6000 BC –
Birch	Sub-Arctic	Pre-Boreal	8000 BC –
Park–Tundra	Arctic	Late-Glacial	10,000 BC –

Table 1.   Forest types as shown by pollen deposits in peat bogs

Rainfall

So far as the references in history go, from Julius Caesar to the present day, Wales has ever been a humid green country, especially on the west side. Well over 100 inches (2,540 mm) of rain, and sometimes double this figure, per annum, fall on Snowdon (in 1912, 246 inches at 2,500 ft above Glaslyn). But on the low-lying coast nearby at Llandudno, the Lleyn peninsula, parts of Anglesey, Flint and the border country with Salop, and the coasts of Pembrokeshire and Gower, the rainfall is much lower, as little as 30 inches (762 mm) in some years.

As the prevailing westerly wind sweeps in from the sea it gathers moisture, forming spectacular cloud masses, which drift in from the Atlantic. They pass over the coastal fringe without much precipitation, but seem to gather ever more darkly upon the cool mountain tops, whether one looks at them from the

Atlantic or the inland side. By the time the wind has carried
them westwards into England they have lost most of their bulk
and density in rain. The sunniest region is the land of the Welsh
Marches, the border line between Flint and Hereford, with the
low coast of the south-west (Pembrokeshire and Gower) not far
behind but subject to occasional sea-fogs.

Snow gathers on the higher mountains late in winter, chiefly
in January and February. In Snowdonia, but rarely elsewhere,
snow drifts remain until April, even May at times. But even so
ski-ing is an uncertain sport in Wales, where sudden mid-winter
rains in a mild spell can wash snow and ice completely from the
high tops. In some winters there is little frost on the coast. Peter
Benoit kept a record of frost at Barmouth over seven winters
and found a minimum of 7, a maximum of 27, and an average
of 20 frosts. But if winters are mild, so are summers: shade
temperatures in Wales very rarely reach 27°C (80°F), except in
inland suntraps. At breezy St Ann's Head, Milford Haven, the
average monthly temperature is just above 15·5°C (50°F), with
February the coldest month (42·5°F) and August the warmest
(59·4°F).

Wind is strongest on the west and south coasts, westerly gales
often reaching 80 mph; an exceptional hurricane on 18 January
1945 sent the anemometer at St Ann's Head to its limit of 113
mph. Stormy cyclonic weather usually begins with a south-east
wind bringing rain in a few hours, then strong winds veering
slowly to north-west bring clearing skies. Anticyclones, bringing
fine days but often hazy sunshine, are marked by north-east
winds, cold in winter but warm in summer, from the land mass
of England.

Humidity is high and constant, as might be expected of the
oceanic climate with sea and mountain mists and cyclonic rains.
As you proceed higher up the backbone of the Welsh mountains, the temperature drops with altitude, an effect most marked
in the spring, when you can leave the coastal strip green and
bright with early flowers—primrose, violet, celandine, dande-
lion, scurvy grass—and find the upland lanes and pastures still

brown and devoid of flowers. An interesting map of floral isophenes in Wales was drawn up by Professor E. G. Bowen (figure
5), using data recorded over the 35 years, 1891–1925, for twelve
common plants and trees first leafing or flowering. These were
hazel, coltsfoot, wood anemone, blackthorn, garlic or hedge
mustard, horse chestnut, hawthorn, oxeye daisy, dog rose, black
knapweed, harebell and greater bindweed.

The method was to take the average date of flowering of each
plant or tree over the 35 years; then take the average of the
twelve. A considerable mass of observation was involved, cover-

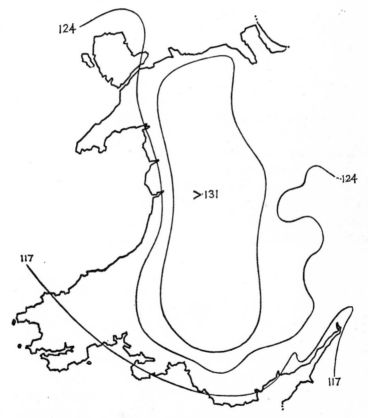

Figure 5   Average floral isophenes 1891–1925

ing the records of approximately one observer to each ten-mile square over the whole of Wales. The figures 117, 124, 131 represent the number of days from (and including) 1 January, so, ignoring 29 February, they are respectively 27 April, 4 May, 11 May. The little map shows clearly how spring comes first to the south-west, to Pembrokeshire and Gower and the rim of the Severn coast; and in fact the detailed records show that all twelve trees and plants are well advanced in Pembrokeshire before 27 April, by which date the early potatoes are beginning to cover the arable fields there with their green haulms. This county can easily compete with Cornwall in commercial exploitation of this early onset of spring; and the early potato crop is highly profitable in Pembrokeshire today. Just occasionally it may be retarded by a late frost, but more often it is the not infrequent spells of dry weather in April and early May which may prevent bulking of the tubers. To counteract this many farmers irrigate the crop from artificial ponds specially constructed to hold winter rainwater; and these ponds are today a welcome feature to the naturalist, with their opportunities to study aquatic wild life, including water plants, birds and insects.

Figure 5 also shows that that spring is at least two weeks later in reaching the uplands of Wales, and it is many days past 11 May before the same plants are leafing above the 1,000 ft contour, and farmers are able to turn out their young cattle, kept in the byre over the winter, to graze on the mountain.

CHAPTER TWO

A natural history of man in Wales

Primitive settlers — Builders in stone — Druids — Animal mythology — The exterminations

OF ALL MAMMALS, man has most influenced the superficial appearance of the land, as described in the last chapter. From the moment he learned to use implements he became the dominant animal, cutting down the native forests, bringing other animals into subjection, enclosing the land around his fortified settlements, and cultivating plants selectively.

Primitive settlers

It is in the limestone caves that we find the first evidence of man inhabiting the land of Wales, more or less in its present form, at the end of the last severe glaciation. The action of carbonate of lime in the cool climate of a cave is to arrest decay, to fossilise. And while earlier evidence of man's settlements and hunting camps in the open during the warm periods between each of the four Ice Ages is hard to trace, and survives chiefly in fragments of worked flint scattered over the land, there is plenty of material in the Welsh limestone caves to show that man of the New Stone Age occupied these at the period when the hairy mammoth, woolly rhinoceros, reindeer, cave bear and musk ox roamed Britain. Their bones are mingled with his, and with his

29

implements of bone and ivory—under the accumulated deposits of later centuries.

Complete fossil remains of Stone-Age man are rare in the world, but a unique part-skeleton—once famous as 'The Red Lady of Paviland'—was uncovered in 1823 in the Goat's Hole cave in the limestone coast of Gower, Glamorgan. From the presence of what was believed at the time to be a bracelet of mammoth ivory pieces it was assumed to be the skeleton of a woman buried in Roman times, and that her kinsmen had dug up from the floor of the cave antediluvian elephant tusks and made ornaments from them. In 1912 experts decided that the skeleton was that of a male, aged about twenty-five years, ceremonially buried in the extended position under red ochre and in deliberate association with a mammoth skull. Many hundreds of Palaeolithic stone implements and ivory artefacts have been unearthed at Paviland, so that its great age cannot be doubted. In 1967 a team from the British Museum of Natural History were able to apply the test of radiocarbon A1 dating to the skeleton, more certainly ageing it at 18,460 ± 340 years Before Present = 16,510 BC. Writing in *Antiquity* in 1968 K. P. Oakley concludes, 'This is by far the oldest human skeletal material which has been radiocarbon-dated on internal carbon.' The 'Red Lady' was after all contemporary with the northern European mammoth which lived close to the edge of the last glaciation.

The forests had fully returned to the low lands of Britain by the date of the enislement, about 6500 BC, from the rest of Europe. But the hill tops were comparatively bare of trees, and from their camps here the stone-age people still hunted brown bear, wolf, wild boar, beaver and deer in the forests and swamps of the valleys below, although the mammoth, cave bear, musk ox and reindeer had vanished from the British Isles.

Builders in stone

With the approach of still warmer conditions about 2500 BC new colonists came to the coasts of Britain, sailing in small boats from

the Mediterranean via the Iberian peninsula, Brittany and Cornwall. They were dark-haired, with long narrow skulls. Like their
Egyptian forbears they were skilled in the art of handling great
blocks of stone. Their religion included the practice of burying
their chieftains in huge chambers of stone, locally known in
Wales as cromlechs, and consisting of three or more enormous
upright slabs supporting a broad capstone (this often over ten
tons weight), the whole covered with a mound of smaller stones
and earth, and having a passage entrance with a portal sealed,
when not in ceremonial use, with a great block of stone levered
into position.

Many of these cromlechs have been destroyed by tomb-
robbers, farmers and others who carried off the stone for building purposes, but often the great uprights and the capstone were
too difficult to shift; and scores of examples of these open cromlechs can be seen today throughout Wales. A few are still
covered and in excellent condition.

In another 500 years came a second invasion across the sea: a
fair round-headed race from Europe, to be known to archae-
ologists as the Beaker Folk from their distinctive flat-bottomed
pottery. They were an active pastoralist people, intelligent
enough to outwit and dominate the resident neoliths. They
buried their dead separately, in round barrows, and were the
first to use and trade in metal tools, chiefly of bronze and copper
from mines scattered over southern Britain and Ireland. They
knew gold also, and sought it in Wales and Ireland.

Evidently there was a fairly steady trickle of Beaker settlers
invading Britain from their settlements along the lower Rhine.
Their encounter with the long-heads seems to have been less one
of fighting and extirpation than of fusion of the two races, probably through the taking of wives and slaves from the conquered;
and the round-heads, with their superior arms and arts, assumed
the priesthood governing both. The many stone circles found in
western Britain were apparently erected at this time during the
long spell of centuries of fine warm weather. They are especially
numerous in Wales. In effect they are laid out like the points of

a compass, with each upright stone throwing a shadow according to the position of the sun in the sky. They were in fact temples where the sun-god, the giver of life, so strong and constantly shining at this period over Britain, was worshipped—as ever in the pagan religions.

Greatest of these British stone circles is Stonehenge on Salisbury Plain; and perhaps the most remarkable feat in connection with the building of this sun-temple is the truth, discovered by the geologist H. H. Thomas in 1923, that thirty-three of the stones forming the inner ring are from natural rock outcrops exposed upon the Presely Mountains of Pembrokeshire. These are the famous bluestones from igneous Ordovician sources (page 14), rhyolites and dolerites found nowhere else but Presely. It is presumed that they were dragged on rollers or sledges over the land, then rafted along the coast by the slaves organised by the priesthood. The so-called sacred altar stone of Stonehenge is likewise from Pembrokeshire, from the micaceous sandstone beds at Cosheston, which lies beside the inner tidewaters of Milford Haven, a convenient point for loading a barge; this fact suggests that all the material from Pembrokeshire was taken by sea along the coast in fine summer weather, probably as far as the Bristol Avon river, and then overland to Stonehenge, a long journey of about 170 miles. The much heavier Sarsen Stones of the outer ring were dragged from sources only twenty-five miles from Stonehenge.

It is fascinating to speculate for a moment on the reasons for transporting the huge rock monoliths from Pembrokeshire to southern England. But we should remember that about this time gold had been discovered in the west, particularly in south-east Ireland. From the heights of Presely on a clear day the Wicklow Mountains of Ireland are visible, where this gold was then mined and worked. We know that traders brought the gold by this shortest route of forty miles across St George's Channel; and we can be sure that this traffic would be exploited by the local chieftains and priests, the Beaker people of Presely. For gold has ever represented wealth, and wealth power, to all races of men.

Acquiring wealth, power and slaves in this corner of Wales the local priests (who were also chieftains, or sons thereof) endowed Presely and its rock outcrops, by their familiarity with the natural bluestone quarries, and by using the rock slabs for their ritual practices, with all the magic powers of life and death and the *tapu* of their cult. So the bluestones became sacred; and it is not difficult to imagine that their transport to Stonehenge was accomplished as a transaction of the highest religious significance between the wealthy priests in charge of this profitable western base and those entrusted with the building of a great new sun temple on Salisbury Plain, that vast prairie where thousands of cattle, goats and sheep were grazed in the sub-boreal period.

About 1500 BC came traders in bronze, using leaf-shaped swords. They placed the cremated ashes of their dead in cinerary urns under round barrows, which are found conspicuously along hill tops and highways in Wales. They probably spoke Goidelic, the ancestral language of the Gaels of Ireland and Scotland, of modern Erse and Gaelic.

Druids

Welsh as a language was brought a thousand years later with the arrival of the Celts, a fair-headed people originating from Barbarian stock far to the east, at least as far as the Danube, and possibly the Russian steppes. In trying to explain the origin of the Welsh people whom he so much admired Borrow wrote lyrically of their revered chieftain whose name is still sung in bardic gatherings in Wales:

'Many will exclaim who was Hu Gadarn? Hu Gadarn in the Gwlad yr Haf or summer country, a certain region of the East, perhaps the Crimea, which seems to be a modification of Cumria, taught the Cumry (the Welsh) the arts of civilised life, to build comfortable houses, to sow grain and reap, to tame the buffalo and the bison, and turn their mighty strength to profitable account, to construct boats with wicker and the skins of animals, to drain pools and morasses, to cut down forests, cultivate the vine and encourage bees, make wine and mead, frame lutes and fifes and play upon them, compose rhymes and verses, fuse minerals and form them into various instruments and weapons, and to move in masses against their enemies, and finally when the summer country became overpopulated led an immense multitude of his countrymen across many lands to Britain, a country of forests in which bears, wolves and bisons wandered, and of morasses and pools full of dreadful *efync* or crocodiles, a country inhabited by only a few savage Gauls, but which shortly after the arrival of Hu and his people became a smiling region, forests being thinned, bears and wolves hunted down, efync annihilated, bulls and bisons tamed, corn planted and pleasant cottages erected.'

The Druidic priests of the Celtic invaders were soothsayers and arbitrators. They interceded with the gods on behalf of their clients, and with ceremonial invocation of their deities made sacrifice in the sacred groves of oak and yew. They taught the continuity of life beyond the grave, which inspired their warriors to be fearless in battle. They buried their dead with the weapons and goods necessary to continue life in the other world. Roman writers have described the austere ritual of the white-robed Druid, who would climb into the sacred oak to cut mistletoe with a golden sickle. In default of a human victim two white bulls were sacrificed, burnt and eaten (Pliny). Tacitus wrote of how the 'heroic' legionaries of Paulinus in AD 61 destroyed the blood-drenched groves of the Druids of Anglesey, along with the howling priests and the witch-like black-robed women aco-lytes carrying firebrands. The Romans were not prepared to tolerate a religion which could inspire revolt against them.

Animal mythology

The Celtic people were good naturalists, well versed in animal lore. They attached to the natural observed behaviour and cries of birds, beasts, and other wild life, divine and prophetic mean-ing. Many of these superstitions persist today in modified form. The flight and calls of such fine birds as eagle, raven, owl and crane (heron) could be interpreted as messages of joy or warning from the gods. Bird names were bestowed on mighty chieftains: one such was Benigeddfran (Blessed Raven), mythological

Page 35 (*above*) The pine marten is largely arboreal by inclination; (*below*) greater horseshoe bat

Page 36   (*above*) A winter haul-out of moulting grey seals, Pembrokeshire;
(*below*) week-old grey seal in white natal coat

prince whose marvellous achievements are described in the Welsh book of legends, the *Mabinogion*. The names of smaller birds of meaner habits—such as the carrion crow, magpie, jay and sparrow—were associated with mean persons, miserable hags, thieves and loose women.

Of mammals the wild boar, *Sus scrufa*, which provided such splendid sport in the hunt, and delicious eating when roasted, is the animal par excellence of Celtic culture, appearing on coins, utensils, carvings and ornaments of stone and metal. Probably the last wild boar was killed in Wales in the sixteenth century; but herds of tame swine were grazed in Welsh woodlands and fattened on acorns in the autumn as late as the early nineteenth century.

The wolf, *Canis lupus*, and bear, *Ursos arctos*, figure in Celtic mythology as wild beasts preying upon man, child and domestic animals. Occasionally a man was turned into a wolf; also wolf cubs were reared in captivity, to act when adult as protectors of the property of princes. There is the famous bad wolf of William Spencer's ballad which attacked the cradle containing the infant son of Llywelyn ap Iorworth and was slain by the faithful hound Gelert, in turn killed by his returning master in rage before he discovered the dead wolf beside his unharmed sleeping child (a legend which appears in the folk-tales of many countries, and is much discredited by historians in Wales).

The wolf may have lingered until late in the sixteenth century. There are many place-names in Wales bearing the Welsh word for wolf, *blaidd*. The brown bear vanished from Wales very much earlier, probably before the tenth century, but its Welsh name *arth* lingers on in place-names such as Aberarth, Arthog, as well as in personal names such as Arthur, and Arthenos or Artgenos (Son of the Bear).

Deer feature in the oldest Celtic stories. The antlered stag, remote, beautiful and noble, was revered as a supernatural beast, and it had the power to lure the hunter into the other world altogether. Giraldus Cambrensis reported herds of deer on the Black Mountains of Monmouthshire, about 1120. Humphrey

C

Llwyd in 1573 recorded red and roe deer seen in 'great numbers in the high mountains' of Merioneth and Caernarvonshire.

The exterminations

The Welsh people were great hunters, however, and with the continued extensive destruction of the ancient forests, as Wales became more densely populated, the forest-loving red and roe deer were completely exterminated by the end of the seventeenth, or first part of the eighteenth century. This was partly due to overhunting, and partly to the increasing pressure to graze sheep and cattle on the mountains, where the last of the red deer sought refuge. It is strange that the forest-loving roe deer did not survive in the deep wooded dingles so numerous in Wales, as it managed to do in English coverts and Scottish pine-woods—where nevertheless it had become scarce a hundred years ago. At the present time roe *Capreolus capreolus* are rapidly increasing in southern English counties where there has been extensive new planting of conifer forest; but they are still very rare or absent in Wales.

At the time of writing red deer *Cervus elaphus* exist in Wales only in a few parks, and the occasional escapees have so far not bred successfully in the wild. The handsome fallow deer *Dama dama*, with its spotted coat and palmate antlers (adult buck only, September to March), has however escaped from several parks, and although not originally native to Britain it now breeds in small numbers in the more wooded parts of Wales, particularly in plantations in Merioneth, Carmarthenshire, and along the border with England.

Truly wild goats are not native to Britain, although goats have been associated with Wales since written records began. Perhaps for this reason a long-horned white goat is maintained as the pampered mascot of the Royal Regiment of Wales. The first goats were probably brought with sheep and other domesticated livestock by the early human settlers from the Mediterranean. Large flocks were herded by the pastoralist beaker folk, and these contributed to the destruction of the ancient forests, as already mentioned.

The pedigree of the present feral stock in Wales today is obscure, but the horns resemble those of the Persian wild goat *Capra hircus aegagrus*, which had been domesticated thousands of years ago, and its milk, flesh and hide utilised by the nomadic peoples moving north-westwards across Europe long before the Christian era. A recent survey of the surviving feral flocks in Wales (Milner and others, 1968) shows them to be limited in size. The estimates are: 20 individuals on the Rivals (Yr Eifl), 90 on the Glyders, 40 on Snowdon, 20 on Moelwynion, 90 on Rhinog, 32 on Rhobell Fawr (all in North Wales); 20 on Cader Idris, Merioneth; and a few surviving precariously on cliffs and crags elsewhere, from domestic stock escaped or turned loose within the last hundred years. In the last category was a small herd of white goats on the steep cliffs of the peninsula of Dinas Island, north Pembrokeshire, which I used to farm; most of this group were billies, and as they became a nuisance to arable crops during the late war they were destroyed by the local agricultural committee's pest-control officer.

The environment of Snowdonia, where the main concentration occurs, is a tough one climatically, and the rate of density is obviously low. So is the rate of reproduction: twins are rare (though common in well-fed domestic goats), and the female does not breed until she is at least eighteen months old. In a cold spring many young kids die. Human activity, including the keeping of sheep on the better, lower pastures, drives the shy, formerly much hunted feral goat, to live hard and high up in the bare crags. Here the Welsh mountain billy, with his noble sweep of keeled, wide-spreading horns, adorns the skyline with a bold majestic appearance. His long shaggy coat is usually of black and white; occasionally a dominant billy is hornless. The nannies have smaller, more upright, spiked horns. As they climb nimbly in the most difficult rocks, by narrow footholds, the wild goats graze indiscriminately and destroy some of the rarer mountain and alpine plants. Goats have never been popular with botanists, and perhaps it is just as well that their numbers are few, other-wise the rare plants of Snowdon, such as the unique Snowdon lily *Lloydia serotina*, might be rarer still.

Without doubt the Welsh people found the beaver *Castor fiber* a useful, sizeable animal to kill for food and fur. At one time it ranged through the wooded valleys of Wales, building its dams in order to flood the adjacent slopes and make easy the felling and transport by water of its sapling food. When one area was exhausted of suitable food trees the beaver moved on to fresh scenes where it could engineer new dams, and thus as it migrated from one artificial lake to make another it acted as a conservator of water, checking run-off of silt. But as it dozed away the winter in its moated lodges it was easily killed by the determined hunter walking across the frozen beaver lake. Its coat was of course at its best in winter.

There are various folk tales of the beaver; in Wales it was known as *afanc* or *efync*, (see page 34), literally the water monster: also as *llostlydan*, which means the broad-tailed one—from its spatulate tail—and one story, taking as its source a Dark Age legend, claims that the beaver caused a great flood in the Conway valley, after the bursting of one of the dams there. The great Welsh prince Hywel Dda (Howell the Good), who died in AD 950, made laws in which the value of a beaver pelt was already high—120 pence as against 8 pence for an ox skin. At the time of Giraldus's visit to North Wales in 1198 it had already been wiped out, but was still present in the river Teifi in Cardiganshire, and this seems to be the last record of the beaver in the British Isles.

The wild cat *Felis silvestris* was one of the last predatory mammals to be exterminated in Wales, less than two hundred years ago, although there have been sight records in the present century. None of the latter however has been accepted by the pundits. The truly wild cat is distinguishable by its numerous fine black stripes running at right angles to the spine, tiger-wise, and by its bushy truncated tail. In contrast, the domestic tabby has a blotched black pattern, some stripes parallel to the spine, and a pointed tail; and although I have occasionally seen feral cats with right-angle stripes along the whole body, the tail has always been finely pointed. Possibly the last pure-bred wild cats in Wales mated with gone-wild or night-roaming domestic cats, and produced offspring closely resembling the pure wild parent. Today most feral cats in Wales (and there are far too many to please the gamekeeper and naturalist) are all colours and patterns. Only in Scotland does the typical *Felis sylvestris* survive in rough upland country like its former haunts in Wales.

CHAPTER THREE

Wild mammals in Wales today

Fox and badger — Mustelids — Insectivores —
Bats—Rodents—Seals

AMONG THE TRULY wild mammals found in Wales today, the red fox *Vulpes vulpes* is universal, and as numerous as it has ever been. Because of alleged depredations among sheep and poultry, but especially new-born lambs, it has been persecuted, hunted, shot, poisoned and otherwise killed without stay; in Wales, over 100,000 foxes were officially recorded as killed between 1949 and 1962 by pest officers and their assistants. Yet recently the species seems to have increased, boldly entering villages and towns at night, scavenging for waste (I have seen a fox push up the lid of a dustbin, in the light from my car), hunting rats and taking offal at rubbish dumps. One admires its cunning and resilience, as one may admire its beautiful lithe form and rich reddish colour.

One of the fox's favourite refuges is the cliffside, both inland and marine. Here it can be found basking on the rocky terraces in sunlight, but when disturbed it will run like a goat over steep inclines where a man dare not follow. Ever resourceful it will dig for grubs and beetles, and other small life, in the sandy soil of burrows from which rabbits have been exterminated by myxomatosis.

One of the surprises following the ravages of this disease has been the fact that foxes have increased rather than diminished in the virtual absence of rabbits locally, possibly due to the cessation of the use of the gin-trap, since this instrument was banned by law in England and Wales about the time that myxomatosis appeared in Wales. These horrible steel-jawed traps caught many foxes, as well as other animals, as they trod on the earth covering the trigger-pan and the trapper of course always killed them, both as enemies of his trade and for their skins. We are now fortunately back to the situation of the last century before the general commercial use of this trap, when rabbits were not a serious pest, but almost an asset (for the sportsman and pot-hunter), and were, as they now are, thinly distributed over the countryside, and kept in check largely by natural predators; although myxomatosis (page 57) still reappears in some recruited populations, and apparently is now endemic.

On the whole, foxes are beneficial to the farmer. They keep down rabbits, rats, voles and mice. I have never known one to attack a live sheep, but they freely eat or carry off dead, or sickly or dying, small lambs which cannot defy their inquisitive approach; such lambs are in any case worthless to the shepherd (who seldom bothers to bury them, knowing that the fox, badger or dog will clean them up). Of course foxes do attack poultry on free range near their cover, especially when feeding cubs; the answer to this seems to be that poultry should be locked up early each day, and preferably at all times kept behind fox-proof netting—poultry at large are a great nuisance to crops and gardens.

The fox inhabiting the higher mountains in Wales is considered to be larger and greyer, and more of a lamb-snatcher: *milgi* or greyhound fox the shepherds call it, to distinguish it from the smaller redder lowland *corgi* or cur fox. Certainly there is very great variation in size and colour of our Welsh foxes; there may be local races, but it must be remembered that colour and size vary much with the sex and age of the individual. The vixen is usually smaller than the dog fox, slightly paler, brush less white at tip, and coat thinner; her average weight is 12 lb, about 3 lb lighter than her mate.

Probably the red fox's success in modern times is due to a combination of three factors: its cunning and boldness in seeking food, its omnivorous diet (while preferring flesh it will eat fruit, grass, berries, insects, grubs, fish and carrion), and its ability to produce a litter averaging five cubs a year, the first litter when the vixen is only one year old.

Less spectacular, less often seen by day, and producing only one litter of two or three cubs annually, the badger *Meles meles* is nevertheless a prosperous member of the Welsh fauna. It too seems to have increased of late, most likely because of a better climate of opinion in its favour as a result of research into its habits and food. It now seems astonishing that this attractive little bear-like creature, with its white-striped snout and endearing domestic habits, should ever have been cruelly 'baited', as was the bear in medieval times, by setting dogs upon it in an arena, for man's amusement and the making of wagers. At one time its flesh was esteemed for food; and I have talked to Welsh gipsies who have told me how delicious a roasted badger ham can be. A few badgers are still dug out from their sets here and there in Wales, by men who keep small terriers specially for fox and badger digging, and chiefly by shepherds when hunting the upland foxes. But in general badgers are left alone today; their greatest mortality at the hands of man is from death by collision with fast vehicles on the road at night.

In Wales badgers inhabit every kind of country, except the land above about 1,500 ft, provided there are dry slopes and banks into which they can burrow deeply enough. Generally they prefer deciduous woods and copses on sloping ground, hedgerows close to cover, and rough overgrown field banks; but they will inhabit the new conifer plantations while these are still young with plenty of undergrowth. Most of the wilder sea-cliff slopes in Wales are frequented, especially those with scrub cover. Once they have established a really large set, badgers are difficult to dislodge. When I first lived at Orielton (page 194, now a Field Study Centre) badgers were established under the large stables block there and had for many years resisted all attempts to evict them. It was amusing to stand on the cobbled floor at dusk and listen to the snuffling and scuffling noises under your feet as the family party prepared for their nocturnal prowl; and by looking out of the stable window you could watch undetected their emergence. Often a bundle of bedding first appeared, for the badger likes to spring-clean the set at intervals; then, lit up by the weak stable light to which they had grown accustomed, the inmates came forth, and spent some time in scratching every part of their fur, sharpened their claws on an adjacent tree-trunk, the young ones playing bois-terously together, the older individuals trundling off to pay the usual visit to neat sanitary pits dug at a salutary distance in the shrubbery.

From each badger set well-worn trails lead to favourite feed-ing grounds. On leaving such a trail a badger will at intervals 'set scent' (as most of the mustelid family do) by momentarily squatting down to deposit droplets of a yellowish oil from musk glands near the base of the tail; this serves as an olfactory signal, believed to guide this nocturnal animal back to the home trail after feeding, to indicate the extent of its territory, and to adver-tise its presence to other badgers. As the boar will sometimes deliberately set scent upon its mate, it also has sexual significance. Badgers have very poor sight and will not recognise an observer if he stays perfectly still until they have got the scent down wind; they find food at night by their extremely sharp sense of smell. They eat prodigious quantities of worms on damp nights; the stomach of a badger which I found newly run over on the road was packed full of the setae and earth of worms. But they are completely omnivorous, as brown bears are, eating berries in season, acorns, beetles, grubs, and any small rodents they can dig out, especially the nests of young rabbits, and carrion.

There are several instances in Wales of new housing estates built on land where badger sets have existed from time im-memorial, but the badgers have refused to leave, creating the interesting situation of 'back-garden badger sets'; and in one instance at least, near Wrexham, the four-legged inhabit-ants have come regularly to food placed under the back-door light.

Mustelids

Eighteenth and nineteenth-century records of gamekeeping and churchwardens' accounts show that bounties were paid on the killing of 'vermin' such as foxes, badgers, cats, and smaller predators. There are references to polecats and woodcats (*cath goed*), and just plain wild cats. It is interesting to speculate whether the *cath goed* was in reality the pine marten, *Martes martes*, as much a lover of woods as the true wild cat, but a comparatively rare animal in Britain. Between 1874 and 1902 gamekeepers on the Penrhyn estates near Betws-y-Coed killed 2,310 cats, 98 polecats, 13 martens, 464 ravens, 16 peregrines, 1,988 kestrels and 738 sparrowhawks. Least numerous on this formidable slaughter list, the marten has nevertheless survived to this day. It is an extremely shy animal, rarely seen, by nature preferring a woodland territory of large area, and therefore individually spread thinly over suitable country. It is an expert tree-climber and is now considered to be not uncommon in that same wooded area around Betws-y-Coed, where it finds cover in the considerable new plantations, (where gamekeepers today are rare or absent), and in south to mid-Wales; but is seldom recorded in South Wales (figure 6).

Foresters encourage the marten because it preys much on rabbits, rats, voles, mice and squirrels which are harmful to trees. Wales indeed should be proud of protecting this beautiful mammal with the intelligent-looking face, large round ears, long chestnut or darker fur, creamy throat, bushy tail and black forepaws; for it exists only in Wales, the north-west Highlands of Scotland, the Lake District (very rare) and Ireland. In default of forest cover it will live in scrub among the rocks, where I have glimpsed it in the wild parts of Sutherland, and western Ireland, but have never had the good fortune to see it in Wales.

However, I have several times seen a mammal which at the time of writing is entirely confined to Wales: the polecat *Putorius putorius*, sometimes called the foulmart or foumart from its habit of emitting a foul stench when alarmed (by contrast the marten was known as the sweetmart, evidently because it had no unpleasant smell). The true polecat is a ferret-like creature with black and white face, short ears edged with white, and longish black coarse over fur, yellowish beneath. A small more reddish variety is frequently recorded from one of its main strongholds, Tregaron Bog in Cardiganshire.

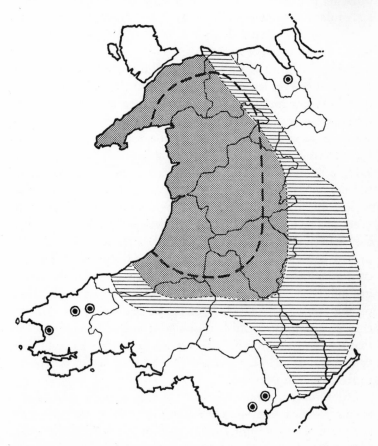

Figure 6 Distribution of pine marten (within the ellipse – – –); of the polecat (dark area: common; ruled area: less common; circles: single records of wandering individuals)

The polecat likes open country broken by rocks, bogs and scrub. In Wales it seems to live much by hunting marsh and aquatic life, including frogs, eels, fish, rats, water voles, moorhens and water birds and their eggs and young. It freely hunts rabbits, but is too large to enter the burrows of smaller rodents, and compared with the marten is a poor climber of trees. I have seen it in dunes, and up to 1,500 ft in mountain rocks. Most often its presence in an area is noted—for it is an extremely active night hunter—on the road in the light of a car's headlamps, and it is often killed accidentally then as, dazzled by the glare, it fails to move in time.

Figure 6 shows the present distribution of the polecat in Britain as a breeder confined exclusively to Wales. Records outside Wales are of strays, and sometimes prove to be escaped ferrets when experts examine them; but it is certainly a great wanderer, and in South Wales has been recorded at least fifty miles from its regular breeding grounds.

Here in the 'polecat zone' of central and north Wales the polecat may be more numerous than the stoat *Mustela erminea* which, during the great rabbit-trapping epoch of the first fifty years of the present century, was virtually exterminated from the western seaboard counties of Wales. The stoat is still scarce in these counties, but gradually increasing. It was and still is more common in the eastward border counties, and on the higher ground. Occasionally the stoat may turn white, or partly white, on the Snowdon heights, as of course it does regularly in the colder climate of Scottish mountains; and it has been shown that stoats which are normally brown in winter can be induced to moult into the white ermine coat by long artificial exposure to freezing temperatures.

More numerous than any other mustelid, the weasel *Mustela nivalis* is fairly common everywhere; but varies in numbers, and apparently is most numerous in years when voles reach plague proportions in upland and forest habitats. This is probably because the weasel is the only mustelid to have two litters in the same year, each producing up to eleven young per nest, and the

Figure 7 Polecat (drawn by Charles Tunnicliffe)

young of the first litter will, in favourable food conditions, breed in their year of birth.

One non-native mustelid must be mentioned. The American mink *Mustela vison* was imported to Britain in 1929 for the purpose of fur-farming. Almost inevitably individuals escaped from their cages, but little was done to tighten up the regulations about preventing these escapes until it was realised that mink were attacking the sacred trout and salmon of expensive river beats. Too late regulations were introduced to make compulsory an outer mink-proof fence around the cages containing the stock of such fur-farms. One or two of the earliest mink farms were established in Pembrokeshire, which may explain why, for the last twenty years, mink have been breeding in Pembrokeshire and the adjoining counties of Cardigan and Carmarthen. Salmon and trout fishermen are very angry about this; though one more philosophic Isaak Walton tells me he thinks that the mink have reduced the numbers of brown rats, water voles and moorhens on a stretch of the river, three species which he believes to be harmful to young fish. Naturalists wonder what effect the mink will have upon the numbers of otters and polecats, which compete for much the same food.

So far, despite a reported general decrease in England, the otter *Lutra lutra* seems to be little changed in numbers in Wales. It is found, though rarely seen, visiting all clean rivers, canals, large ponds and lakes; and it also frequents the coast, where it feeds on inshore fish, flounders and the inhabitants of rock-pools. The Ishmael of the water world, it travels incessantly except when nursing its cubs in some holt in the rocks or tree-roots overhanging water. When I was operating the Orielton Duck Decoy, Pembrokeshire, otters paid occasional visits, much to be dreaded by any decoyman, since they will enter the duck traps, kill the ducks, then bite their way out through the wire-netting. One night they even tackled and killed nesting Canada geese, which normally will drive away human visitors. However, there were long periods with no trouble from the otters, and the year in which a pair reared a family on the Decoy Lake was, strangely, free of raids on wildfowl. The decoyman had an explanation: 'Animals never hunt close to home. Would betray their young if they did. I've noticed rabbits will live in the same burrow as a fox with cubs!'

There are one or two packs of otter-hounds operating in the summer in Wales; but it is doubtful if these can have any serious effect on otter numbers, since a kill is comparatively rare. More are killed by water bailiffs; and many fishermen in Wales still persecute the otter at every opportunity. One morning a young otter came out of the sea at Tenby and padded up the main shopping street, to the amusement of some, the alarm of the fearful, and the wild excitement of small boys and ignorant men. Hunted with sticks by the last it was brutally killed, cowering behind dustbins outside Woolworth's. Too late I found its sleek, beautiful, battered body hanging behind the town dustcart, and sent it to the National Museum of Wales.

Insectivores

Handbooks of mammals usually place the order *Insectivora*, containing the hedgehogs, moles and shrews, first on the systematic list, because they exhibit many primitive features suggesting an early appearance in the time scale of animal evolution, close to the earliest primates. The hedgehog *Erinaceus europaeus* leads the British list of insectivores. Archaically known as the urchin (meaning goblin), the hedgehog is most remarkable physically for its top coat of hair which has developed into thick sharp-pointed spines. Each spine has a knob-like base, resembling a pin-head, inserted in the thick layer of muscular tissue which by contraction enables the hedgehog to roll itself into the well-known ball, leaving only the radiating spines in view. This defensive mechanism protects it from many enemies, but fox and badger are said to be able to open and kill it, occasionally leaving the skin as proof. The tawny owl can sink its talons through the spiny coat, and tear the hedgehog open, and the polecat is said to be able to worry it until it opens in sheer exhaustion. But domestic dogs and cats quickly lose interest in the spiny ball, which may be the reason why the hedgehog is most numerous in large gardens and suburban parks, where it is unlikely to be troubled by fox or badger; it is also often protected by gardeners because of its appetite for slugs, insects, mice, and other horticultural pests.

In Wales the hedgehog is common in such situations, and comparatively rare in wooded, thinly inhabited country, although well distributed below the 1,500 ft contour. It seems to prefer open farming country well supplied with hedges where it can find cover; also orchards, and commons with furze; and it can be found in sand dunes, feeding on snails, which it seems very fond of. In the mild coastal belt of Wales it is often abroad in mid-winter, usually not in fat condition; unable to hibernate then because of the mild weather, it may well be unable to find sufficient food either.

Another remarkable small mammal of the same order, the mole *Talpa europaea* is found abundantly throughout Wales, even—where there is enough soil for burrowing—on the highest mountains to 3,000 ft. But as it was a late colonist in western Europe after the last glaciation, it did not cross to the offshore islands. There are no moles in Anglesey, Bardsey, Skomer, Skokholm, etc—just as there are none in Ireland, the Isle of Man, Orkney and Shetland.

The three typical British shrews are present in all counties of Wales. The common and pygmy shrews, *Sorex araneus* and *Sorex minutus*, are numerous even on Skomer Island. The lesser shrew can be caught in the same live traps with the common; and although both species feed on the same insect and other invertebrate food of the top soil and litter layer of their common habitat, the pygmy shrew does not burrow like the common shrew, which has almost mole-like vigour in swiftly driving its runways in the soft top layers. The pygmy shrew uses these runways, and also those of mice and voles; and on encountering other species its defence is to run away, or if cornered it utters an intimidating high-pitched screaming (studies in captivity). It is a nimble climber, ranging into bush and tree-cover at night in search of spiders, insects (but rejecting insect larvae) and woodlice.

The pretty black-and-white water shrew *Neomys fodiens* is found—though rarely seen—on all clean waters of any size in Wales, on ponds, lakes, streams and rivers, in marsh-drains and other open-ditch sites, especially in wooded country. It has been trapped far from water in the undergrowth of woods. Swimming under water, it can look like a silvery fish due to the air bubbles clinging to its fur, as it hunts for water-snails and crustaceans; but most of its activity takes place at night. It is said to be able to paralyse large prey, including earthworms and snails, with bites which inject a poisonous secretion from the sub-maxillary gland.

Page 53 (*above*) Red kite at nest; a photograph by Eric Hosking, taken in Spain. Photography of the few surviving kites in Wales is forbidden; (*below*) chough at nest

Page 54 (*left*) The water-ouzel or dipper is resident along all fast-flowing streams and rivers of clear water; (*right*) a typical Welsh upland bird: pied flycatcher at nest

Shrews live at such a high speed that it is believed that they die of old age at eighteen months. Unlike moles, which can live for at least three years, all British shrews die in the autumn of their second year, at the end of their breeding season, leaving only the progeny of their two to four litters (4–7 in each) to survive the winter. Except when breeding they are solitary. They are able to store food in their burrows. They are able to re-ingest their faeces, by eating them direct from the everted rectum, a habit which may be useful when they are short of fresh food; but in cold frosty weather, it is presumed that the immature shrews must hibernate in order to survive at all, since their pulse rate and general metabolism in summer is so rapid that they may die of starvation if unable to find food equal to roughly their own body weight each twenty-four hour (Crowcroft, 1957).

Bats

Bats come next in the systematic order; and Wales is reasonably well supplied with nine of the twelve species recorded in England. These include the greater horse-shoe bat, *Rhinolophus ferrumequinum*, which I have found in small numbers in the limestone caves of Pembrokeshire and Gower, and it is also recorded from Merioneth. The lesser horse-shoe bat, *Rhinolophus hipposideros*, is more numerous and widespread over Wales. A large colony lived at my former home of Orielton; and on summer evenings it was amusing to watch these bats enter the house and hawk usefully after moths and flying insects under the lofty ceilings of this gracious old manor. Here too I have caught the whiskered bat, *Myotis mystacinus*, which is fairly widespread in Wales, but sometimes confused with abundant pipistrelle, *Pipistrellus pipistrellus*, or the less common Daubenton's bat, *Myotis daubentoni*, which I have never had the luck to see alive, although it is recorded particularly from north Wales, and rare in south Wales.

Natterer's bat *Myotis nattereri*, and the noctule *Nyctalus noctula*, have been recorded from most counties in Wales, and are pos-

D

sibly more common than is supposed, especially in well-wooded areas. (A noctule was caught in a mistnet set for storm petrels on Skokholm, 12 September 1968.) The barbastelle *Barbastella barbastellus* has only been recorded from Radnorshire, and as long ago as 1904; it is an almost black bat, with ears close together at top of the head. Diligent search for this and other rare bats in old houses, caves, hollow trees, old mines and tunnels along the border with England would be worth while, for bats have been little studied in Wales. I have marked, by wing-banding, groups of lesser horse-shoe and pipistrelle bats at Orielton, and this work continues there to the present day.

Pipistrelles wander far in warm weather in summer, even flying out to the Pembrokeshire islands of Skomer and Skokholm in broad daylight then, evidently strays from some of the very large colonies which can be seen issuing from old buildings and roofs at dusk on the nearby mainland. The long-eared bat, *Plecotus auritus*, with its extraordinary ears up to two inches in length, is less numerous, and although found in every county, seems to prefer more sheltered situations, hunting on the wing through tree tops, its huge sound-catching ears directed forward to echo-locate small flying prey.

Rodents

The rabbit *Oryctolagus cuniculus* is not a true native of Britain. Originally confined to the Mediterranean region it spread northwards, aided by artificial introduction. It is thought that it was introduced by the Normans, who brought rabbits with them from France, perpetuating their own feudal right of *coneygarth*—keeping rabbits in warrens. The famous Norman-Welsh squire of Pembrokeshire, Giraldus Cambrensis, mentions rabbits when writing about hares in Ireland in 1186. The Earls of Pembroke, who held the islands of Skomer, Skokholm and Middleholm from the early thirteenth century, evidently established rabbits there, so ideally suited with light sandy soil for burrowing and no ground predators. When Earl Aymer died in 1324, the value of his estate included the rabbit profits of these islands at £14 5s yearly, a goodly sum in those days. The skins were an important article of export at that time.

Rabbits on the mainland of Wales were, however, quite scarce until well into the nineteenth century, spreading but slowly from the coastal strip. When gin-traps were first used on a commercial scale in the present century, rabbits began to increase at a phenomenal rate, for three principal reasons: these traps were inefficient to exterminate; they killed out the many natural predators which, in normal pursuit of rabbits, entered more burrows than the individual rabbit did, and consequently were more liable to be trapped; and the trappers, finding a remunerative living by the use of gin-traps, made sure they left behind sufficient breeding stock to provide even larger catches in the following year. As rabbits snowballed in numbers, the demand for trappers increased, until at last these men were able to dictate terms for their services, offering a lump sum for the winter crop of rabbits on each farm, a sum which might even pay the farm rent but did not compensate for the damage the rabbits caused to pasture and crops. Between 1928 and 1954 the deterioration of agriculture in the western coastal counties, especially Anglesey, Caernarvon, Cardigan and Pembroke, was enormous. As an example, far more rabbit meat was exported (1,460 tons) in 1945 from Pembrokeshire than the total in that year of sheep, pig and veal meat sent from that county. The climate of these maritime counties suited this Mediterranean animal more than that of the cool wet inland counties; but farmers were deeply disturbed also by the great increase in rats resulting from the trapping of stoats and weasels, which had become very scarce (page 48).

Suddenly in 1953 the virus of myxomatosis, nearly 100 per cent lethal to rabbits, reached south-east England, following its artificial introduction in France in the previous year. As a farmer and naturalist, I was invited by the Nature Conservancy to investigate its progress and vectors, and discovered that the main vector in Britain was the rabbit's own flea, *Spilopsyllus cuniculi*;

and that farmers from far and wide were transporting sick and dying myxomatous rabbits to their land from the infected warrens in England. Suffice it to say here that the first outbreak in Wales was in Radnorshire, induced by infected fleas deliberately brought from Kent.

It was somewhat ironic that with other naturalists I had for over twenty years been working to secure a law prohibiting the use of the gin-trap; but that when the Pests Act making gin-traps illegal in England and Wales was at last passed in 1954, there were hardly any rabbits left. Myxomatosis had done the trick so thoroughly that even the few healthy rabbits caught were unsaleable; no one who had seen the gruesome effect of the disease had the desire to eat rabbit. This was really fortunate, however, in that it meant that farmers were obliged to treat the unmarketable rabbit as vermin. Rabbit control committees were set up in each county to check any reinfestation, using legal humane means of killing.

Although rabbits are still present in every county in Wales, they are now very much scarcer. Like influenza in man, myxomatosis is now endemic, reappearing from time to time whenever rabbit numbers increase locally. The virus, which in Britain is transferred from healthy to sick rabbit on the mouthparts of the rabbit flea, tends to lose its lethality, and more individuals are becoming immune; but mortality remains high and at least fifty per cent of rabbits still die where fresh outbreaks occur. As mentioned earlier in discussing fox numbers, mammals which prey on rabbits have increased since the abolition of the gin-trap, and altogether, with farmers taking greater interest in controlling rabbits on their land (now a statutory obligation in case of re-infestation) through local committees, the rabbit remains generally at a satisfactorily low level of population—satisfactory in the general sense that many countrymen enjoy seeing the odd rabbit about, even though no one mourns the simultaneous decline of the rat.

The brown hare *Lepus europaeus* is a true native of Wales, but has never been as numerous as it is in the rolling and flat lowland pastoral and arable lands of England. Early in this century the rabbit-trapper caught many hares in Wales by placing traps in their open runways, in hedge-gaps and under gates used by hares. One Pembrokeshire trapper claims to have caught the last hare in the county in the winter of 1927–8, and certainly no hares were reported there for the next thirty years, when a landowner near Haverfordwest put down some imported stock, which have slowly spread elsewhere. Generally the brown hare survived through the lean gin-trapping period in Welsh–English border country, where to some extent it was preserved by game-keepers in a drier climate and on uplands more suited to its taste than the wet western counties. The blue or mountain hare *Lepus timidus* was introduced from Scotland in the last century, and still survives in small numbers, chiefly about the high ground of Snowdon. Any hare seen below 1,500 ft is likely to be the brown species.

Typically the red squirrel *Sciurus vulgaris* is a native inhabitant of coniferous woodland, or forest where conifers are dominant; but in the absence of any other squirrel competitor it ranged thinly through the native deciduous woods in Wales, especially where it could find acorns and nuts. It was fairly common even in isolated woods in open country, such as Orielton and Little Milford woods in Pembrokeshire, and Glasfryn in Caernarvonshire. Its disappearance from these and many other woods in Wales coincided with the great increase and spread of the grey squirrel *Sciurus carolinensis*, introduced from America into Britain by many releases between 1876 and 1929. By 1954 the grey was reported from all western counties of Wales save Anglesey, although mostly as isolated individuals. A survey of red squirrel distribution 1944–5 (Shorten, 1954) had shown the native species was present in well over 50 per cent of parishes throughout Wales (100 per cent of parishes in Brecknock and Montgomery; nearly every parish in Merioneth and Radnor shires) but it has since greatly decreased, and at the time of writing is locally fairly common only in Anglesey, where the grey is still rare; and in the conifer plantations and some higher mixed woods in central and North Wales where it is unusual to see a grey squirrel.

Monica Shorten states that there is no firm evidence that the grey persistently drives away the smaller red species; but the grey has a preference for deciduous woods, and observation suggests that once the grey enters a wood with a preponderance of non-coniferous trees, the red disappears. The journal *Nature in Wales* records many interesting examples of the spread of the grey squirrel, which is shown to make an extensive westward migration in some autumns. Individuals can be met, ambling along open country far from trees, and it has been seen on cliffs in Pembrokeshire where, one would have thought, it would be vulnerable to attacks by hawks. The grey will, however, take cover in rabbit burrows, where near Tregaron in 1965 one was killed in a fight with a ferret underground. Grey and red squirrels have come to the same food at a bird table in Denbighshire.

One can only hope that the grey squirrel will follow the population trend of many another introduced species by settling down to a lower level of numbers in ecological balance with the native fauna; and it is possible that this is now taking place. At least grey squirrels are not so numerous in south-west Wales as they were ten years ago in 1960. Red squirrels can still be locally common: in 1966 they were reported in 'considerable numbers and causing some damage to young conifers' at Llangammarch Wells.

Three species of vole are common, each in its special habitat, in Wales. The bank vole *Clethrionomys glareolus* inhabits country well covered with vegetation, from deciduous woods with ground cover, to hedges in more open country and bushy heathland. This reddish attractive little beast climbs with agility, and I have frequently live-trapped it by day. The field or short-tailed vole *Microtus agrestis*, a stockier greyer species, with a much shorter tail, is obviously not adapted to climbing, and is strictly terrestrial, preferring open country with thick low cover. It ascends to the highest mountain tops where grassy cover exists; but it can also be trapped in new plantations where the grass is still long, and here it may riddle the ground with its burrows, and cause damage to the young trees. Periodically it has outbursts of population; there was a particularly severe one in 1955 following the virtual extirpation of the rabbit by myxomatosis. In the resulting thick ground cover voles bred up to plague numbers in some mountain and forest sites by the winter of 1956-7. Young conifers of all kinds, and oak and ash saplings, were barked (girdled) around the roots and main stem, causing losses up to 60 per cent of total trees recently planted. Usually this huge population dies off in the hard weather of late winter, suddenly, and few voles are left; but during such a plague many predators feed well: kestrels, buzzards, hen harriers and owls appear in larger numbers than usual throughout the winter.

Although bank and field voles can be taken together in the same traps set in suitable sites on the mainland, it is unknown for both to co-exist on small islands. Thus on Jersey an insular bank vole is found, only; and on Guernsey only a field vole, which also is subspecifically distinct from the mainland vole. In Wales Skomer has only the bank vole, which, because it is larger and lighter in colour than the mainland bank vole, has been given the subspecific scientific name of *skomerensis*. This has been lately challenged by mammalogists who consider that the old idea that it is an isolated relict population of a once widely distributed species is wrong, and that instead, like other isolated island populations of small mammals, the Skomer vole is derived from ordinary mainland bank vole stock, possibly brought over accidentally by the settlers who built the Iron Age enclosures about 2,000 years ago. This explanation of its ancestry does seem feasible: small mammals, breeding rapidly several times in a year under conditions of isolation, are able to make rapid evolutionary changes in a few hundred years. The rabbit on Skomer and Skokholm for instance, introduced in Norman times, is already visually quite distinct in having a blacker pelt, and is about ½ lb smaller than the mainland rabbit. P. A. Jewell suggests that the handsome, bright-coloured Skomer vole should be scientifically referred to as *Clethrionomys glareolus* (Skomer).

Figure 8   Skomer vole (drawn by Charles Tunnicliffe)

Skomer, treeless, and with its low vegetation usually over-grazed by thousands of rabbits, is really a typical field vole habitat; although before the introduction of the rabbit, it was most likely covered with bushy scrub and wind-bent trees suit-able to the bank vole. However, in the absence of the field vole the bank vole thrives on this island in long grass and bracken habitats, where it is hunted by buzzard, kestrel, short-eared owl, raven and the gulls. Here too, after periodic outbreaks of myxo-matosis, when rabbits are low in numbers, the voles increase with the extra grass available, and with them the numbers of breeding pairs of short-eared owls.

The water vole *Arvicola amphibius*, sometimes called the water rat, is more than twice as large as the other voles. Its chubby form, not unlike that of a half-grown brown rat, can be seen by most rivers, large ponds and ditches in Wales. In the autumn, after a good breeding season, the young voles disperse and wander, and may be met with far from water, or beside tiny streams and springs not suitable for making a permanent home. After a severe winter few may survive; and there may then be several years of building up numbers again, as after the winter of 1962-3, which was followed by a dry summer in 1964. Cors Tregaron is a stronghold of this vole.

The handsome bold-eyed wood mouse *Apodemus sylvaticus*, also known as the long-tailed field mouse, is very common in almost every kind of habitat, from bare screes on mountain tops and cliffs on offshore islands to sheltered woods, but is most numerous in the last situation. Trapping on Skomer has shown that the wood mouse there is extremely hardy, living in rocks down to sea-level, and because of its long isolation it has, like the Skomer vole, developed differences such as heavier weight, less yellow on the breast, and it also has larger litters than the mainland wood mouse. It does not apparently compete with the abundant Skomer vole, but occupies for shelter the numerous stone hedges and natural rocks, ranging much farther afield for food than does the vole. But it will not, apparently, tolerate the presence of the house mouse *Mus musculus*, on a small island, if we are to judge from the fact that as soon as the inhabitants of St Kilda left that island in 1930, the house mouse quickly died out, leaving the wood mouse in complete possession. If ever house mice have lived on Skomer (and it seems most likely that they were accidentally introduced there during periods of farming and corn-growing) they must have died out when from time to time farming ceased, and with no artificial cover and food available in the empty farm buildings, they could not compete in the wild with the field mouse. On Skokholm the house mouse, accidentally introduced, is the only mouse: it thrives, in the absence of the wood mouse, in all situations enjoyed by the wood mouse on Skomer, including the hedge-walls and in the cliffs down to the high-tide zone; but might disappear if ever the wood mouse was introduced.

The even more handsome yellow-necked mouse *Apodemus flavicollis* is significantly larger than the wood mouse, and has a broader yellow chest spot forming a collar contrasting with the whiter belly. It is thinly distributed in Wales but has probably been much overlooked, living in woodland and well-timbered districts. It is fond of fruit, and can be trapped in orchards; and enters apple stores in winter. It has been recorded from all counties except those of Anglesey, Caernarvon, Flint, Glamorgan, and Pembroke.

The charming harvest mouse *Micromys minutus* can even more easily be overlooked, which may be why it has been so seldom recorded in Wales, although present in some border counties. Remains of harvest mice have been found in pellets at a barn owl roost in Vaynol Park, Caernarvon, 1968.

The house mouse, already mentioned, needs no comment on its world-wide distribution commensal with man and his buildings. Yet it is probable that it was absent or rare in Wales before the Roman invasion and the settlement of peoples in permanent buildings. It is Asian in origin, and still lives successfully wild in the steppes of that continent. But as we have seen, it seems to suffer in competition with the abundant wood mouse in Britain. Although it can be trapped hundreds of yards from buildings, especially in late summer and autumn, and will infest standing ricks of corn and hay, it is not common except in or near inhabited buildings. Recent research (R. J. Berry, 1967) on a marked population at Skokholm confirms my general experience when living there for twelve years: there is a huge build up of numbers each summer, for the young mice born in April begin breeding in July, and these young individuals range over the whole of this 240 acre island in search of food and nesting quarters. As soon as cold wet winter weather comes the mice retreat to buildings and the cover of rocks and cliff crevices. From a peak of 4–5,000 in autumn Berry finds they drop down to as few as 150 surviving in buildings and cliffs, all of them under a year old; there is a complete turn-over of population annually.

One of the earliest references to rats in Britain is that of Giraldus Cambrensis who in his *Itinerary through Wales*, undertaken in 1188, refers to a man in Pembrokeshire who 'suffered a persecution from rats' which sought to devour him. Giraldus was engaged in that year on a tour of Wales with Archbishop Baldwin to enlist Welshmen to join the (third) Crusade for the relief of Jerusalem. It is often stated that the first rat to arrive in Britain was the black rat *Rattus rattus*, and that it came with the armies and ships returning from earlier Crusades. Later it brought with it the Black Death (bubonic plague) which struck Wales severely in the fourteenth century.

In the eighteenth century the brown rat, *R. norvegicus*, arrived, a much hardier, larger northern beast living more on or under the ground, where it has since supplanted and driven the black rat to the higher parts of old buildings, storehouses and wharves. There is an oft-quoted early record of the brown rat in Wales in a letter from William Morris to his brother, the scholar-poet Lewis, from their Holyhead home in August 1762, complaining that he 'had three men reaping all my corn and not a little trouble did we have, Norwegian rats devouring it standing. That particular tribe was not here when you were living in our district.' Lewis Morris left Holyhead in 1750; so most probably the brown rats invaded Anglesey from ships calling in at Holyhead between 1750 and 1760.

The brown rat flourished for another two hundred years, and the black rat declined. By 1960 the latter was reduced to small colonies in the centre of Cardiff, and possibly a few other sites in Wales. This decline is not entirely due to interspecific competition with the brown rat; both have been spectacularly reduced by modern methods of control and hygiene in both town and country. The black rat is nearing extinction in Wales, and the brown species is found chiefly in grain-growing areas in the country, and in urban storehouses, rubbish dumps and sewers.

The dormouse *Muscardinus avellanarius* is very local in Wales, confined to sheltered inland woods with scrub cover or coppices, especially where honeysuckle abounds, for this pleasant squirrel-like mouse will seek nectar from the flowers and strip the fibrous bark to line its ball nest. W. M. Condry has seen it feeding by day in Wales, but normally it is nocturnal. Summer nests are in bushes, thick hedges and other tangled growth well above ground. In winter it hibernates, and is then usually solitary. I have examined one hibernaculum, which was in the form of a perfect ball of honeysuckle bark interwoven with long grass, the whole dry and neatly hidden in a fork of bog myrtle, over which dry molinia grass had formed a perfect natural waterproof thatch, although the ground below was a typical bog myrtle swamp; in such a situation the sleeping dormouse is less likely to be discovered by prowling animals which might prefer not to flounder about in a winter bog.

Seals

Last but not least of the mammals of Wales are the seals. Their human-like faces and voices have given rise to tales of mermen and mermaids. Although popular in legends of Scotland and Ireland, seals figure rarely in those of Wales. This may be because Welshmen have traditionally never been much interested in the sea, having no boats save the one-man skin (now canvas) and lath coracle for taking salmon in their rivers—although with the nineteenth century the men of the developing coast settlements began to enlist in the merchant service and some became successful captains of sail and steam ships. Also, as all larger wild land mammals had been exterminated in Wales several hundred years ago, we can be pretty sure that seals were ruthlessly slaughtered by the protein-hungry Welsh people whenever they could find these animals along the coast.

Thus seals were rare in Wales right up to the present century; their chief resort being the caves and islands off Pembrokeshire, and to a lesser extent the exposed coasts of Anglesey and Caernarvonshire. When the inshore fishermen acquired guns in the last century they killed seals for the sake of their skins and blubber, and also because of alleged damage seals caused to their nets. Wealthy landowners and their guests went seal-hunting, principally as a sport. For example, there is a record of Lord Kennedy killing seals in Pembrokeshire for trophies. He shot seven and was pleased with his sizeable bag (suggesting they were scarce at that time, about 1889); he records that he 'never saw a male exceeding eight feet'.

A seal that length could only be a grey seal *Halichoerus grypus*; the smaller common seal *Phoca vitulina* never exceeding 6½ ft. In any case the common seal is very rare in Wales, and has only been recorded exceptionally; it is difficult to understand why, since it is found all along the coasts of Ireland 50–60 miles away. I have seen many hundreds of grey seals, but only one recognisable common seal, in Wales. Seen close to, the adults are easily distinguishable, the common having a slightly dished face, short from nose to brow, and the nostrils lie close together, very like those of a cat or rabbit; the coat, brown-grey, is densely covered with black spots, more uniform than the larger blotches of the grey seal's pelt. But the young seals up to two years old are less easy to identify, for there is great variation in colour and markings, especially in the grey. Nor is the habitat much help: the common seal may lie out upon rock and sand alike; but the grey prefers a rocky coast, and seldom lies out on sand, yet like the common seal it will swim far up the sandy estuaries of salmon rivers in search of fish.

Thanks to the creation of island nature reserves in Pembrokeshire and to the Grey Seals Protection Act 1932 (with penalties since increased) this seal has become more numerous, and can be seen, for the looking, along the whole western coast of Wales, and occasionally well up the estuaries of the Severn and Dee. The main breeding herds are concentrated in Pembrokeshire. In the two largest sanctuaries of Ramsey (about 200 pups born annually) and Skomer (not less than 50 pups each year) grey seals are now delightfully tame as a result of long protection; and local boatmen run trips in summer, taking visitors to see them basking on the low-tide rocks and beaches. Another 100 pups are, on average, born annually on beaches hidden in deep caves or under unscaleable cliffs along the rocky coast of the same county. A very few are born elsewhere, under the cliffs of Cardigan, Caernarvon, and Anglesey. At all times numbers of adult and subadult grey seals lie out over low tide on reefs off Bardsey, the Skerries (Anglesey), Grassholm and the Smalls lighthouse (Pembrokeshire), and elsewhere. There are at the present time about 2,000 adult and subadult grey seals in the whole of Wales, this figure excluding pups less than six months old. It has been my good fortune to make a detailed study of this population (Lockley, 1966).

Seals like to bask in the sun, but their lives are regulated by the moon in that they are active or passive according to lunar time. Over high tide they fish; then as the tide falls they drag themselves out to rest and sleep on favourite beaches and reefs. It is amusing to find that older seals return time and again (like club members to a favourite armchair) to their individual niche on beach or rock where, if they find a younger weaker seal in possession, they drive it off—usually by a display of bared fangs and hissing snarls. Except where they have been unvisited by man over long periods they do not like to remain too far from the sea (on a low spring tide perhaps), and are watchful if they expect human visitors, shuffling nearer to the water as the tide drops, ready to make a quick getaway. Unable to walk on land like the sea-lion (which doubles its hind flippers beneath its body), the seal is awkward when ashore, dragging its useless 'tail' (hind flippers) along, slug-fashion, and can easily be overtaken by a man running along a beach, or climbing over boulders, if surprised more than a few yards from the water.

If for this or any other reason the grey is unable or unwilling to come ashore to rest it can and frequently does sleep in the water. In shallow water it will sink to the floor of the sea, rising about every five or six minutes to the surface to breathe and re-oxygenate its blood, an automatic process during which it does not necessarily open its eyes, though it may do so. After about a dozen deep inhalations of air, its nostrils close, having expelled most of the air in its lungs, and, losing buoyancy, it sinks without effort and still apparently asleep. If there is a heavy swell running which would disturb its sleep on the bottom it will sleep in an upright position (known as 'bottling') at the surface, remaining buoyant by retaining some of the air in its lungs, with its nostrils opening and shutting at regular intervals, its eyes closed most of the time. (This answers queries about the diving behaviour of seals made by people who have been puzzled by the appearance and disappearance of seals they have seen from Welsh cliffs.) You may also be lucky enough to watch a seal bring a large fish to the surface, and devour it piecemeal, holding the body of a skate or conger-eel in its mobile front flippers, and tearing off mouthfuls. Small fish are swallowed under the water. It is not certain how seals locate their fish prey when the water is cloudy with sand or mud; but as one can meet totally blind seals in fat condition, sight is not essential, and probably hearing and the highly sensitive facial whiskers provide the information and orientation needed in darkness.

A fairly reliable guide to distinguishing the sexes is provided by coat colour and markings: the mature bull is much darker than the cow, with lighter spots and blotches; conversely the cow is lighter, with dark spots and patches, often also on the belly, and her head profile is straighter than that of the bull, which has a convex one. However, there is great individual variation, with occasional very pale bulls and black-brown cows. A further complication for the unwary is that after lying in the sun and wind for an hour or two the coat changes colour as the sleek wet overfur dries out, and the buff underfur shows, so that at a distance a grey seal appears at times almost white, especially if it exposes the paler belly to be dried out. Adult male greys rarely exceed 9 ft in length and about 500 lb in weight; adult male common seals average about 5 ft, and weigh around 350 lb; mature cows in both species are up to one-quarter smaller.

The grey seal cow drops her pup (the old-time seal-hunters dubbed the young seal 'pup', and this term has stuck in spite of attempts to replace it by the more logical term 'calf'; certainly the baby seal has a dog-like face) between September and November. In Wales the majority of births take place in the last fortnight of September. More rarely a few are born in the spring, and occasionally in any month of the year. The cow seeks a beach under high cliffs or inside a cave above normal high water mark. Parturition is rapid, and the mother, without licking her young or touching the afterbirth, encourages the white-coated pup to suck the fat-rich milk oozing from her (two) teats, which are situated low down on the belly. Seal milk contains 50 per cent fat—6 per cent fat is the maximum in the domestic cow.

The pup is at first weak and thin, and does not willingly enter the sea. It seems indeed to fear water, and with good reason: many a feeble new-born pup is killed, despite attempts by its dam to protect it, by heavy seas sweeping the rock-bound beaches during high tide over an onshore gale. It grows rapidly, putting on weight at the rate of 2–4 lb a day and storing fat in the form of a coat of blubber under the long white natal fur. In a few days the pup is strong enough to swim buoyantly and enjoys doing so in fine weather. However, some pups, born well above the high water mark, may not go to sea at all during the short lactation period of three weeks normal for this seal. These fortunate few remain where they were born, with, or regularly visited by, their dam. They complete the moulting of the white birthday fur, which falls in a ring around the fat sleepy creatures. The second coat is dapple-grey and usually well grown by the time the cow deserts her pup between the third and fourth week. In that short period the pup has often trebled its birth weight of about 30 lb; and the cow has lost some 100 lb—for she has never been seen to feed herself while suckling her child.

Nor is the breeding bull seen to feed. He is too occupied with guarding the cow or cows which have come into his self-appointed territory of one or more nursery beaches. As soon as

Page 71 (*above*) The ring-ouzel is a regular summer visitor breeding in the upland dingles of Wales; (*below*) redstart at nest: another Welsh upland bird

Page 72 The gannets of Grassholm: (*above*) part of the gannetry of 15,000 nests; (*below*) the nestling being fed

the first pup is born the bull stays close to the mother, usually patrolling the water inshore, alert to drive away rival males. The cow is ready to mate about 10–14 days after parturition. Occasionally the bull will lie at rest on the beach at low tide, especially after mating, which is normally in the sea, the pair remaining united for up to an hour, during which they may fall asleep at intervals, either afloat or under water.

The master bull rushes into the sea at first sight of another bull invading his territory or approaching his cow or cows; with snarls and if necessary hard bites he drives the intruder away. The size of his territory varies considerably. Depending on the number of cows using a large beach he may have to share this ground with other bulls because he cannot physically both defend a long beach and attend to all its nursing and potentially oestrous cows. Such a beach is Abermawr at the back of Ramsey. But in Wales most bulls have to operate on small beaches which are easily controlled; and many bulls only enjoy a single cow in one small isolated cave. There is ever a surplus of younger or secondary bulls ready to serve an eligible female when the master bull becomes thin and spent with his exertions, and his long fast, and relinquishes his territory. Virgin cows of course have no nursery problems, and are mated at sea by younger or non-territorial bulls, with whom they can be seen playing on or near local beaches, tide-swept and unsuitable for nursery purposes, which seem to be used exclusively for general resting and assembly.

Mating so soon after parturition seems to be a useful adaptation, a form of insurance, in a sea-wandering species; the male is able to find the female more surely while she is tied to nursery duties. But the true gestation period is much shorter than the time of mating implies. Although fertilisation of the ovum occurs at mating, implantation and development are delayed. The fertile ovum remains free in the uterus for some four months. Because of her recent pregnancy, lactation with fasting, and then the annual moult, the cow is too exhausted physically to support a growing embryo. By March the moult is complete

E

and with a good coat of blubber restored by heavy feeding, the true pregnancy of seven and a half months begins; the tiny blastocyst attaches to the wall of the uterus and becomes a growing foetus.

Studies of grey sea pups born in Wales and marked with numbered flipper tags by members of the West Wales Naturalists' Trust have shown, over twelve years, what is now known to be a typical dispersal movement, which is similar to that of other British herds (Farne Islands, Orkney and Hebrides). Our Welsh pup forsakes its nursery beach about a week after its dam has abandoned it. At this age of four to five weeks it is very fat and can withstand a long fast if it does not immediately find food in the sea. It is interesting that at such a tender age it now makes the longest voyage of its life. Before the end of the year marked Welsh-born pups, two to four months old, have wandered as far as western Ireland, Cornwall, Brittany, and one has reached the north coast of Spain (figure 9).

The recovery in Spain, 600 miles from home, was of a pup born on Ramsey Island ten weeks earlier; so, allowing about half of this period for nursing and learning to be independent at home, it had swum approximately seventeen miles a day, surface speed. A remarkable feat, but this and many other recoveries have shown that while an average migration can be six linear miles in a day, individuals can log up to twenty surface miles in twenty-four hours. Allowing for a good deal of natural deviation, observed of these pups during swimming, the actual distance swum could easily be doubled; and allowing for periods of rest and feeding each day, the speed of swimming must be still further increased. An adult seal which I timed from a cliff top as it swam energetically along beneath me, over a distance which I afterwards measured, was making six miles an hour surface speed.

How long do grey seals live? Unfortunately the metal flipper rings used to mark seals have rapidly worn thin and fallen off after a year or so of sea-wear. But a preliminary first branding with a hot iron of eighteen grey seal pups on Ramsey Island

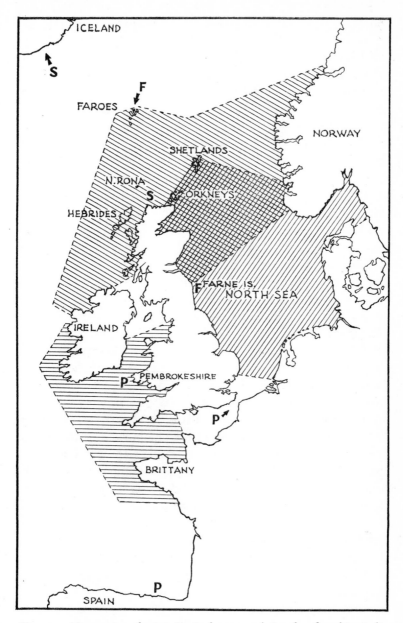

Figure 9 Movement and migration in the grey seal. Results of marking individuals in Pembrokeshire (P), Farne Islands (F), Scotland (S). The
shaded areas show the range of recoveries of about 500 pups; single
recoveries elsewhere indicated by single letters P, F, S.

which our party carried out in October 1946 has so far yielded three sightings, each alive and well, and the individual brand mark still clear enough to read, as follows: a bull in January 1959, about 25 miles NE of Ramsey, therefore 12+ years old; a bull in October 1960 at Ramsey, therefore 14 years old; and a cow at Skomer in August 1967, therefore 21 years old. In captivity the grey seal occasionally lives well over forty years.

In Wales the female is ready to mate at three to four years of age, and is then not quite full grown. At certain assembly places already mentioned young females and males play together a great deal, especially early in the spring, rolling over each other in the surf of a pebble beach, biting, necking, and even mating. It is difficult to understand why mating should take place at this season, unless there is no delay in implantation; in which case a young cow, mated in February or March, would produce her pup about the normal time—September or October. But the spring is a time of great relaxation, the annual moult is over, the wandering pups born last autumn are back home (those which have survived the hardships of winter and migration), the mature bulls have no territorial ambitions except to keep their sleeping niche clear of other seals.

It is then fascinating to study a large herd at rest, for in Wales it consists of all ages, from really old bulls and matrons to youngsters under six months old—the last are wearing a very pale faded coat at this time of year. Usually the oldest seals, like old people, do not play, but spend the time sleeping, each with its head separated from the next by a few inches, ready to moan in protest if a neighbour accidentally touches it in yawning, scratching and turning movements. However, their sociable nature is evident, despite these apparently grumpy threats, in the fact that the herd keeps in a compact group, leaving the rest of the beach empty. From time to time, as the tide recedes, there is a general awakening and a shuffling seawards; then the herd goes to sleep again, except for those young seals which are enjoying play along the edge of the water. When the tide flows and laps the sleeping herd it is reluctant to move, but as the surf splashes their fur, each seal makes an effort to remain dry by hunching laboriously uphill. The seals sleeping in the higher positions resent this encroachment on their siesta space, and snap and snarl, waving a warning foreflipper. The master bulls win this display, and are avoided by smaller weaker individuals; but even the dominant seals must move when the tide reaches them. Many seals now slip into the sea, for this is the time to fish; but others have evidently not had enough sleep, and will haul to the top of the beach and continue the long rest, which may last over more than one high tide.

The songs of the seals are really laments, musical moans for more sleeping space; and when the nursing pup is hungry and seeks to be fed it wails for mother. Seals have very keen hearing; and of course hear sounds under water even better: Arctic and Antarctic seals call to each other in the blackness deep below the winter ice; and it is believed that they catch fish after locating them by 'listening' for vibrations set up by their swimming movements. Stories of seals listening to music played to them on wind and string instruments have given rise to the belief that seals are 'musical'. They are in fact merely curious to locate the source of strange sounds, and soon lose interest when they have done so. They are extremely intelligent, as studies in captivity (Hurrell, 1968) of the grey seal have proved.

Recognition between individuals is, however, less by voice and sight than by individual smell, as anyone will realise who has watched a cow seal seeking her pup in a crowded nursery. She will haul herself along towards the source of her pup's wailing, sniffing and rejecting other pups until she has nuzzled the body of her own child before relaxing and letting her milk flow. The mature bull has a very powerful characteristic smell, quite overpowering in the confines of a cave. I have often detected the presence of seals first by the olfactory clue, when on marking expeditions along the wild labyrinthine rocky shore. I have twice watched completely blind cows in fat condition, each suckling her pup, which she could recognise only by its scent and voice. On each occasion when I approached, silently in rubber boots, the cow got my scent and felt her way closer to her pup until she could nuzzle it and pat it with one flipper. As she could not see me standing near her, but recognised that danger was present, she was reassuring herself that her child was safe. A pathetic scene, yet both these blind cows in their familiar nursery sites subsequently reared a pup in two successive seasons, making their way each time by touch and kinaesthetic memory to the exact spot—which they could not see; and obviously they had had no difficulty in mating, and finding a good living in the rest of the year. I have also encountered blind bulls which were in good condition.

The pup is unsociable in its first year, and avoids other pups almost as soon as it is able to move about after birth, snapping and biting when it accidentally encounters other seals in the nursery. It is imprinted first with the body, scent and voice of its dam, representing the security of a rich food supply. The breeding bull takes no notice of the pup, except to fling it aside if it gets in his way. At last even its own mother deserts it. No wonder, then, that it sets off alone on a long voyage, without a friend in the world!

Even when it returns to the home herd after its first winter of wandering, the six-months-old seal is wary of other seals. It may be another year before, in its second spring and summer, it is able to break down the barrier of individual safety distance, and touch another young seal desirous of play. I have watched these tentative advances in the spring assemblies under Welsh cliffs. They take place at the edge of the sea, between individuals of the same or opposite sex, indiscriminately. The surf games become more sexual in the third spring time, when the adolescent seal is about thirty months old. Males of that age may be seen playing homosexually, or with females; but females of that age seldom play with other females; rather they seem to seek out males of any age, and invite sexual satisfaction by clasping them and wriggling, invitatory movements. Sometimes these young cows will follow mature bulls as they leave the sleeping beach and swim seawards; the old master may allow the young lady to cling to him in the water, but evidently he has none of his passionate fire of the autumn nursery season, he may even seem bored, and a fertile mating in the spring may be rare, even if intromission is successful.

Old beachmaster bulls gradually acquire scar tissue around their thick neck—which develops rolls of wrinkled skin with age—due to fighting rival males in autumn. Probably a bull is at least eight years of age before he has grown large and powerful enough to dominate a desirable nursery of several cows.

CHAPTER FOUR

The birds

Birds of prey – Mountain birds – Lowland birds –
Birds of the coast

IN THE WILD fastnesses of the Welsh mountains, by the vast blue
plain of the Welsh sea, the bird-watcher may seek and find fine
large birds, rare birds, not to be seen in the smooth cultivated
lowland of England too overpopulated by man. He may miss
certain small birds of the south-east on crossing the Welsh
border; but he will find ravens, buzzards, kites, falcons, and
several low highland, but not high alpine, species; and of course
great numbers of sea and shore birds.

There are no resident eagles left. They disappeared from Wales
some centuries ago, and it is rare even to see one on passage—and
if so it would be the migratory sea-eagle, the white-tailed
Haliaëtus albicilla. The Snowdon range of mountains is today too
over-explored by climbers and trampers; the more southerly
high tops may hold more interesting birds for being less frequented by man. The Welsh name for the peak of Snowdon—
Eryri—is significant, however, and said to mean 'the eyrie of
eagles'. Giraldus Cambrensis mentions them in passing Snowdon
during his *Itinerary* of 1188. Leland, travelling for three years
1536-9, found 'Cregeryri Mountaines horrible with the sighte of
bare stones' and wrote of eagles which it is uncertain he ever saw
there. The botanist and London apothecary Thomas Johnson in
1639 was deterred from climbing Snowdon by his Welsh guide,
partly on account of cloudy weather, but also because 'our rustic
feared the eagles nesting there, for they are accustomed to sweep

crosswise on swift pinions before the faces of cattle feeding on the precipices and by suddenly frightening them make them fall down the rocks and become their prey'.

True enough that eagles will swoop at trespassers near their nest, but hardly with deliberate intent of scaring them over the edge. What happens is that cattle, feeding along the fringe of a cliff, seeking the greener herbage there, stray too near the edge; either the edge gives way, or in trying to turn back a beast stumbles or is jostled by another behind it, loses its balance and falls. Cattle are too accustomed to birds to be scared of any that do not actually strike them. But once a beast becomes carrion, eagles and other scavenging creatures eagerly devour the carcase, and are then accused of killing.

Birds of prey*

When Ray and Willoughby made their two expeditions in 1658 and 1662, inspired by Johnson's botanical success, they saw no eagles, which must have died out in Wales about this time. But one predatory bird was to survive down the centuries to the present day in Wales: the red kite, now found nowhere else in the British Isles.

Once despised as a carrion-eating, chicken-snatching thief, this large handsome hawk is easily recognised by its long deeply forked chestnut tail, comparatively narrow, angled wings, and white-streaked brown head. It was once numerous even in the streets of London, where it scavenged the open drains; Gilbert White of Selborne saw it often soaring in the sunlight over English downland (1773). But by 1900 it was confined to remote rainy valleys in mid-Wales, and had become a collector's piece, and its eggs eagerly sought. By 1905 only five individuals were known for certain to be living. A new interest in its protection resulted in a slow increase to ten pairs by 1910. But again there was a recession, although one pair nested in Devon in 1913, and

* The scientific names of birds mentioned in this chapter are given in the alphabetical *Index of Welsh Birds*, pages 203–18.

another in Cornwall in 1920. Only four nests were successful between 1933 and 1937, for egg-collectors renewed their assaults by crafty dawn visits. Stricter new conservation measures were put in hand after the war, with local watchers responsible for each nest; and at last there has been a substantial recovery to about twenty pairs, about half of which usually rear young successfully each summer—at the moment of writing.

Unfortunately there is little likelihood that the red kite will increase much further. Each pair of the little colony surviving in Wales today needs a large hunting territory, where it lives a life very different from that of its London ancestors, or even from that of the red kite in part of Europe and Asia, where it is still a village scavenger, although rapidly becoming scarcer as modern methods of hygiene reduce its carrion food supply. The Welsh kite lives by picking up small birds and mammals, frogs, worms and beetles, as well as eating carrion, chiefly sheep which have died in the hills.

Welsh sheepwalks tend to get larger as the remote hill farms become amalgamated, both for economic reasons and because of the unwillingness of the younger people to live in isolation. Some shepherds now live in valley villages, making their inspection of flocks at rarer intervals than did their forbears living on the hill. As a result the modern shepherd may be unable to find each sheep of his flock in trouble in time to save it. Sheep are prone to many diseases and accidents: they become ill, they tumble on to their back (especially when heavy in lamb) and cannot right themselves, they become fast in brambles and bogs, and in snow. The law of survival of the fittest operates, and if the hill shepherd is unable to rescue a stricken sheep in time, he will know the familiar sequence of its fate. As it grows weaker in its state of immobility the ever-watchful birds of prey, soaring vulture-like in the sky, drop down to inspect it. Usually the first to make the attack on the living sheep are the ravens; they work in pairs—for once mated they remain lifelong partners in all activities. One each side, they hop around the sheep until it is either dead or too exhausted to move head or limbs to drive the birds away. They feast on the soft parts first, the eyes and tongue, and pull the entrails out through the back passage. Meanwhile the kite, if present in the district, together with buzzard, crow and magpie, soon arrive to join in the feast. In that order they may dominate and take a share of the carcase, moving aside after each has become satiated. At night, and even by day in remote situations, the fox will feast until it is glutted. Badgers may eat their share; and often an underfed sheep dog will pay surreptitious visits to fill its belly. Writing from experience as a shepherd in Wales I can add that unless I buried a sheep casualty deep in the ground—not easy on rocky slopes—I would find subsequently that dog or badger or fox had dug down to reach the carcase.

It does seem that this steady supply of sheep carrion from 'natural' casualties in the mountains helps to maintain a good stock of kites, buzzards and ravens there. Often the first intimation of their presence is a distinctive call overhead: the shrill mewing of the kite, the softer plaint of the buzzard, the cronking note of the ravens. On fine days, with warm air rising over a sun-heated valley, you might see all three soaring at great heights together in the same thermal, joined perhaps by gulls, rooks and jackdaws which explore the moors in such weather. One should scan the sky frequently at such a moment, looking for the dark specks of these birds which seem to enjoy the experience of effortless gliding.

Even in its last refuge the kite is still so rare that bird-watchers should keep away from its nesting grounds during its breeding season from early April to July, after which the adults and young birds may be seen over a wide area of mid-Wales, sailing for hours above the hanging oakwoods which are a favourite nesting and roosting site, hunting the little fields in the dingles, or the moorland slopes.

Buzzards, those attractive broad-winged miniature eagles, have increased, after a lean period fifty years ago, and may now be seen in every county, most numerously in central and south-west Wales. The sudden decrease of rabbits due to myxomatosis reduced their high numbers (highest around 1955) in rabbit-infested areas; as for example in the Castlemartin peninsula of south Pembrokeshire where at least forty pairs were counted in the spring of 1956, just after the epidemic, but breeding success in that year was low, and ten years later there were fewer than twenty pairs in that rural district. This is still a reasonably strong population, but in the last few years there has been a slow but definite decline in Wales. Like other birds of prey, the buzzard's numbers and fertility seem to be affected by modern conditions of high farming, particularly the use of chemical pesticides which are absorbed when devouring small animal prey weakened or killed by these poisons. Also, despite protection by law, buzzards are still shot in certain gamekeepered districts; which is a great pity, since they do far more good than harm. They may snatch up an occasional young pheasant, partridge, grouse or duckling, but they live principally upon small rodents, including full-grown rats, half-grown rabbits, and many hundreds of mice and voles.

The buzzard in well-wooded country gets a living by waiting in a tree, or on a rock, wall or post (telegraph posts especially) and watching for a passing bird or moving small creature on the ground. Incautious young crows and magpies, fresh out of the nest, are surprised by the sudden silent pouncing glide. I once saw a buzzard fly from a tree and seize a barn owl which had just alighted on a tennis-net post at Orielton. The buzzard flew low with the prey in its talons, but dropped it after a few moments; and the owl flew off to the cover of the nearby wood. The buzzard followed it, and although subsequently I found only the white, feathered claws of a barn owl in that wood, there was no direct proof that the buzzard had killed it. However, the buzzard's stealthy swoop is not invariably successful. One day, as I was watching a brood of newly hatched mallard feeding on a shallow pond, a buzzard glided down to snatch a duckling. Just before it could strike, the mother duck sprang vertically from cover, alighted on the buzzard's back and brought it down so effectively that the hawk disappeared under the surface of the water! What would have happened if I had not run forward in astonishment and so disturbed the courageous duck, I do not know, but the buzzard might well have been drowned by the infuriated mallard. When rescued, the hawk was in very poor shape; after being placed in a warm room to dry out its plumage for several hours, it recovered and was set free.

Along the coast the buzzard builds in the cliffs (using seaweed at times) but inland it usually constructs its bulky eyrie of sticks, heather, grass and debris, much like that of the kite, high up and close to the trunk of a tree, and often with large bones welded into the structure. A kite will add all sorts of rubbish, and sometimes bright bits of rag; the buzzard regularly brings fresh sprays of rowan, birch, pine and other local plant material to decorate the nest. Each is shy and sly in the breeding season, except when raven, crow or jackdaw pass too close when the hawk will attack, wailing loudly; it has good cause to fear these agile scavengers which will devour the eggs if these are left unguarded. It is better not to approach near enough to put off the incubating hawk: the nimble corvid is apt to visit the nest before the hawk, shy of humans, returns.

Buzzard nests are sometimes found in accessible places, such as the heather and fern slopes above dingle streams (and even, on one occasion, on the chimney of a deserted cottage in such a glen). As soon as they leave the nest, but before they can hunt properly for themselves, the young buzzards mew incessantly, and this wailing hunger cry is especially evocative of Welsh forest and mountain dingle in high summer.

A recent census of the raven in the British Isles shows that Wales is its main stronghold. Along suitable parts of the coast there may be a density of one pair to each mile (as the raven flies—straight as a crow). On Skokholm's 240 acres two pairs may breed, and up to four pairs on Skomer's 722 acres. Ravens also breed freely on crags inland and are common about the precipices of Snowdonia. Where there are no inland crags they will nest in tall isolated trees if these are far from human habitation. Occasionally a pair will alternate between a tree and a cliff nest site nearby. One nest I knew of in the Presely Mountains was in an ancient sycamore leaning over an abandoned hill farmhouse. Another was very accessible at 18 ft from the ground in a beech within an extensive forest plantation.

Studying some seventy nesting territories in North Wales 1946–67 E. K. Allin recorded fifteen nests in trees (thirteen in conifers, two in oaks). A few pairs used the same nest, or one very close by, year after year. He found an average of over five eggs to a nest, of which an average of 3·37 young survived to nest-leaving age, which agrees with my own records for raven nests at Skokholm over thirteen years. In nests above 1,000 ft altitude Allin found slightly fewer—3·12 average—young were reared.

The raven lays its eggs about two months earlier than the buzzard, at times even in February. During incubation the off-duty bird is alert to attack any predatory bird passing close; and later when the nestlings are still small, it develops a positive frenzy of agitation, and has been known to swoop at man. This parental frenzy dies away soon after the youngsters are fledged. The old birds moult, looking very ragged for a while, and neglect their children. These gather in packs in the late summer, and where ravens are numerous—up to a hundred at a favourite roost on Skomer, and up to sixty at mainland roosts. These flocks disperse widely in search of food during the day, but will converge on a rich source of carrion, vulture fashion when a sheep or other farm beast dies in the open. Ravens also congregate at rubbish tips, and slaughter-house dumps, dominating the gulls, crows, rooks, daws, starlings and sparrows in competition for food.

About 1930 there were peregrine falcons breeding along the whole coast of Wales, as well as on crags inland. There must have been well over a hundred pairs nesting about that time. The subsequent decline from about 1940 onwards was due at first to extensive shooting of adults at the nest by the War Department: the falcons were said to be taking too many homing pigeons carrying War Department messages during the 1939–45 war.

Then came a huge and indiscriminate post-war development in the use of chemical poisons in agriculture, for the control of crop diseases and insect pests. As in the case of the buzzard, the peregrine has been affected, but much more severely, by assimilating residual poisons present in the bodies of prey which has eaten poisoned vegetable or invertebrate food. Even if the falcon does not die of chemical poisoning, its fertility may be affected to the extent of laying eggs which fail to hatch (these have been proved to contain lethal traces of poison chemicals), or perhaps not laying at all.

The decline has been extremely rapid. None was reported as nesting in a 1967 survey by observers all over Wales. In 1968 one eyrie in Pembrokeshire was raided, apparently by falconers or their agents, but fortunately the three eyases were subsequently recovered, and reared to fly free and wild at Skomer in that summer. One can only hope that this noble bird will recover some of its numbers, now that stricter control of pesticides harmful to birds has been introduced. Meanwhile conservationists in Wales have wisely ceased to publish details of the few successful breeding sites.

As its name implies the peregrine is a wandering species, often seen in Wales at other than nesting sites, in autumn, winter and spring. It is most frequent along the coast, where it can find prey in the concentrations of ducks, waders and starlings. Some of these peregrines are doubtless on migration to and from northern breeding grounds. One such was a young tiercel (male) watched in pursuit of a starling at Skokholm. When the frantic starling dived towards my house the peregrine failed to pull out of its headlong stoop in time to avoid the stone wall—into which it thudded and was killed outright. On another occasion I saw a cliff-nesting peregrine strike a curlew in mid-air, cutting its head off completely with the knife edge of its clenched rear talons: the severed head fell at my feet, the body tumbled into the sea! This is the typical method of kill: a slashing blow in flight. But I have watched the Skokholm peregrines in playful mood leisurely 'bind' to the slow-flying puffin (its principal and plentiful food there) with opened talons, then release the bird in mid-air so that it tumbled seawards, dazed, but how badly pinched by those scimitar claws I could not tell.

Young peregrines, and perhaps adults when hungry—for the splendid down-flying stoop is quite often unsuccessful—will tackle prey on the ground, such as young rabbits, unfledged gulls and other large earthbound birds which they see moving. I once found a young peregrine dragging a shearwater from under a ledge of rock.

Mountain birds

So far we have mentioned only a few of the larger birds for which Wales is specially interesting, birds which haunt the mountains but some of which also nest along the coast. In this category is a much smaller falcon, the merlin, in habit a minia-ture peregrine in many ways, fast-flying after its chiefly winged prey, tenaciously following each twist and turn of lark, pipit and wheatear, trying to force it into the sky, then rising above it to make the final swoop. However, the merlin does not strike dead, but binds to its prey, the rapier talons piercing the body so that the victim is usually dead by the time the merlin alights and begins plucking. But often the prey, by devious last-minute aerial manœuvre, escapes, or dives into cover. One merlin in pursuit of a swallow was as exhausted as its shrilly calling quarry, and eventually gave up the chase.

Like the peregrine the merlin is a confirmed wanderer, visiting open country everywhere out of the breeding season on its southward migration in autumn, for it is a northern species near the southern limit of its nesting range in Wales. Those we see in winter are probably from breeding grounds in Scotland, Nor-way and Iceland; they haunt the lower ground and the sea-coast, for there is not much small bird life on the mountain then.

Our Welsh merlins take up their summer territory quite late, the male appearing first in April or early May on some chosen moor, heathery cliffside or sand-dune. On a fine day it will

Page 89 (*above*) Manx shearwaters gather off Skokholm at sunset; (*below*) a pair of Manx shearwaters courting outside a burrow on Skokholm

Page 90 Puffins on Skomer Island: a sociable group, one parent carrying fish for the single nestling in its burrow

indulge in aerial display, rising and circling upon a thermal, with buzzards high above. I have found a clutch of eggs in a magpie's old nest in a blackthorn bush; and occasionally it will utilise the abandoned nest of a crow (once on a roofless cottage); but usually the four eggs are laid in a hollow in the ground rounded out by the movements of the hen without much or any attempt at lining. The falcon does most if not all of the incubating, but the tiercel brings her food, chiefly small birds; and she also feeds the new-born eyases. Any bird carcases surplus to immediate appetite may be pushed under the grass near by, or at the plucking site, forming a larder of 'high' meat.

Very few pairs now breed in Wales. Most of its dune haunts I knew as a boy in South Wales have been invaded by camping and caravan interests, quite incompatible with the co-existence of this shy falcon. It still nests regularly in a few lonely mountain and moorland haunts. But although widely distributed it was never common; which is just as well for the lesser birds which it preys upon. It is dismaying to find merlins killing stonechats in dune country, for example, and ring-ouzels and dippers on the moorland. Yet nature seems to arrange these matters on a fairly equitable basis so that in the end the predator lives in equilibrium with its prey locally. The Welsh merlin hunts over many square miles of open country, and although it takes moths and beetles on wing, its principal victims are the numerous meadow-pipits and skylarks.

Of other interesting moorland birds which the ornithologists will want to see in Wales, the ring-ouzel maintains its numbers. Earliest arrivals pass through in March, by coast and inland crag. Summer breeders settle down early in April in the dingles of the higher mountains and the edges of new upland plantations, usually above 1,000 ft. Sparsely distributed, this most attractive mountain blackbird with the white crescent breast is shy of humans, although very aggressive towards other birds. It is a lovely experience to be walking up a mountain glen, often other-wise rather birdless in early April and with few flowers yet out, and hear the persistent short flute of the ring-ouzel, which will

F

sing both early and late to announce its possession of territory and advertise for a mate. And I have heard an exuberant male on migration sing to the sound of the sea on a windswept cliff.

The nest is difficult to find, well hidden in heather or boulders beside a stream, or rarely in a niche in a roofless building; and so secretive are the pair when they see you. Two broods may be reared. In August you will find the family parties feeding liberally on the fruit of mountain ash, bilberry, cowberry, before flying south to winter in France, Spain and the Mediterranean. (Here, as ringing has shown, far too many find their way on to the table of Latin sharpshooters, along with every other kind of migrant bird—even the tiny goldcrest, which I have seen, slung to the belt of a Portuguese 'sportsman', in company with the bodies of sparrowhawk, blackcap, chiffchaff, ring-ouzel, robin and sparrow.)

The ring-ouzel nests in all suitable habitats in Wales; but not in Anglesey; and in Pembrokeshire the mountain blackbird is chiefly seen on migration, although it has bred occasionally in the Presely Mountains. The other ouzel with the white crescent breast, the dipper, is more widely distributed and resident, inhabiting all clear-water streams from 2,000 ft down to sea-level. Occasionally it has built its nest under the arch of a bridge over a river which is salt at high water of spring tides, but it is more plentiful at higher elevations. In summer the dipper moves right up into the mountain glens, occupying territories which are maintained season after season.

In numbers dippers seem to fluctuate considerably: in one summer a stream seems to have a pair every half mile, in another season hardly any. The occasional severe winter with frozen streams, and the not infrequent violent spring spate destroying the early nests, both obviously affect population. Some pairs begin nesting very early, usually the old experienced birds, and as a rule they are wise enough from experience to build their moss nest well above normal flood level. By the time the average bird-watcher visits the mountain streamside in May the first brood may be fledged.

The nests of younger birds, breeding for the first time, are often placed too low, and are swept away. A recent study of dippers by H. Alder has shown that the cock makes several imperfect nests—like the male common wren—within his territory, but it is the hen who decides which shall be used for incubation, and generally the cock is an idle husband, not usually feeding his mate, even during the sixteen long days of incubation which she undertakes alone. The cock is larger than the hen, which is significant in many species as coincident with polygamy, and in fact, where males are in short supply, two or more females may mate with the same cock. But each nesting female keeps to her territory, and fights with any intruding female. As the male cannot easily help feed the young dippers in more than one nest at a time, in that case all the work must fall upon the hen whose nest is farthest from the male's usual water patrol. The female dipper is also, Alder finds, more sedentary than the male, remaining closely attached to her territory until driven out by a younger stronger female, when she seems to disappear—possibly, like so many old displaced creatures in nature, to die of chagrin and sheer homelessness. But any dipper, becoming weak and unwatchful, is likely to be mopped up by one of its several local predators: sparrowhawk, merlin, owl. Jackdaw and magpie may take eggs and young, and escaped mink have become nest destroyers, too.

To counter a high mortality the dipper raises two broods, starting another nest if a first or second is destroyed during incubation. They are admirable, hardy birds: both sexes sing, and their sweet wren-like warble is one of the most pleasurable sounds of the mountainside. From the ancient stone bridges of Wales, you can often look down upon the dippers, busily gathering food by walking under the water, their claws grasping the pebbles, heads bowed to deflect the current and counteract the buoyancy of their body; and they can also be seen taking tiny fish, as well as beakfuls of caddis-worm, mollusc, shrimp and insect food to the nest.

Associated with the dipper, the very beautiful grey wagtail is resident in the same situation of clear running water. It is often confused with the yellow wagtail, but in fact the yellow wagtail is not a visitor to mountain streams—it is principally a summer migrant nesting only in wet lowland meadows in the border counties from Denbigh and Flint south to Monmouth and Glamorgan. Both can be seen elsewhere on migration and if so, distinguishing points are the olive-green back and the rich yellow head of the yellow wagtail; whereas the male grey has a rich black throat (spring only, turning whitish in winter) and the female grey has a white throat at all times. Also the grey wagtail has a longer tail.

Several wading birds enliven the moorland in summer. Of these the common sandpiper is widespread, sharing the stream with dipper and grey wagtail, and the mountain llyn with teal and dunlin. On a rare occasion, this sandpiper might be seen bobbing its pure white breast there as early as March, but usually it arrives in April. As it flies before you it utters a characteristic peeping note. This is repeated in the courtship song, uttered in a pretty display by the male: he arches his wings above his body and spreads his tail. The mated pair are charming in their attention to each other, and to the strikingly beautiful eggs and small chicks. It seems that they normally pair for life, or at least meet and mate again, as long as both shall live, judging by their faithfulness to territory and the same nest site year after year. The nest is usually well hidden by overhanging vegetation near the water (often in the long grass of a railway embankment). Both sexes incubate, and help to feed the tiny nestlings which run about as soon as they are dry from the egg.

The common snipe justifies its adjectival qualification by breeding commonly on the wet areas of heather, moss and rushy peat as high as these are found. The click-clocking vocal noise, and the fantastic instrumental bleat which sounds like a long-drawn call of an amorous billy goat and is produced by the tail feathers in zooming flight, are evocative of the Welsh summer upon high open hill and low wide marshland. Both snipe and curlew nest in these situations, the curlew perhaps more freely on the lower ground. Curlew have definitely increased in Wales, and are nesting in grass fields and commons down to sea-level. Both species return early, even in February, to inspect their moorland territories, the curlews loudly announcing each visit with the ecstatic wailing and bubbling music of their spring song. They may share the moorland territory with the lapwing (peewit or green plover) which formerly nested in large numbers, high up on wet ground, but like the curlew now seems to concentrate more on land nearer sea-level. As many as twenty pairs of lapwing nest on the molinia marsh at Skokholm.

The common redshank is much more local as a moorland breeding bird, but here and there it can be found nesting on damp rushy ground from about 1,000 ft down to sea-level.

The rarest waders breeding on the mountain are the golden plover and the dunlin, both confined to the highest ground where there is plenty of manœuvring room clear of human interference. The few pairs of golden plover which haunt the mountain spine of Wales will be found in the bleak areas of short heather mixed with peaty depressions. The aerial display of the handsome black-breasted male is often the first sign as you cross these upland wastes. Singing his liquid *tooroo-tooroo*, he flips through the sky with deliberate slow wing beats before suddenly diving earthwards. The performance is reminiscent of that of the courting lapwing; but the sexual chase is more prolonged, and the pair, and often a trio, will disappear from sight over the skyline.

Much tamer is the little dunlin, which also has an aerial display, and a sexual pursuit flight. You have only to sit perfectly still for a while on arrival in its feeding territory along the water's edge of a mountain pool to have it walk up to you, as it runs nimbly along, probing the soft ground for worms and larvae; I have many times coaxed a preoccupied dunlin into a narrow funnel of netting pegged down in such a site, when catching waders for ringing purposes. But they are shyer near the nest, which is skilfully hidden in low heather or a clump of grass; the incubating bird will sneak away through the low ground cover on your approach, and presently, if you follow, it will try to lure you from the vicinity by feigning injury, realistically dragging its wings as if wounded as it runs jerkily ahead of you. Satisfied that it has removed you far enough from the nest it then flies away altogether—a trick common to many waders, and some ducks, at the nest, or with young.

Dunlin are very scarce as breeders in Wales, frequenting chiefly certain headwater pools, close to which the nest is hidden. But it is probably the commonest wader haunting the estuaries and salt flats in Wales from autumn to spring.

Two ducks breed on the high ground, beside the mountain llyns and pools: teal and mallard. Provided the pool has enough aquatic vegetation in which it can hide and feed, the teal is content. Several pairs may occupy the same pool, for it is a gregarious bird. Yet it prefers to hide its nest well away from wet rushy ground in the dry cover of heather. The gorgeously plumaged drake leaps into the air and flies out of sight when you appear. But although incubation is by the duck alone, he returns later, and will hang around the nesting ground until the eggs are hatched, and join his mate when she leads her ducklings to the pool.

Much the same behaviour applies to the mallard couple, which will breed in the same situations, as well as almost anywhere else where there is water, down to sea-level, and frequently in quite steep sea cliffs. Teal and mallard are the only ducks nesting on the high mountain pools, but you may see other swimming birds from time to time, some as passing migrants, a very few more rarely breeding, such as the great crested and little grebes. White-fronted geese regularly feed on the high upland bogs and pastures from late October to the end of March or early April, and with them may be a few pink-footed geese. More rarely still wild swans—chiefly whoopers—alight on the llyn in mid-winter during a mild spell when it is free of ice, cheering the ornithologist who has made a visit to the moors at this season of few birds.

The heights can indeed be cheerless and empty on a cold cloudy winter day, when even the resident red grouse seem reluctant to take wing from their sanctuary in the long heather. But on the occasional clear, sunlit mid-winter day it is well worth making a tramp over the mountain while the light is bright. On such an occasion you may see a hen harrier quartering the heath for a day-active vole or other ground prey; or put up small parties of snow-buntings, which feed on the seeds of moorland plants, and the fleshy roots of coarse grasses. Buzzard, kite, raven, gull and often rooks may visit the high ground in such fine weather, although the pipits and small birds will be away.

In summer herring and black-headed gulls regularly hang about laybys and picnic viewpoints on well-used mountain roads; they are almost as tame and cunning as the Welsh ewes which invite you to dispense your crumbs and biscuits, and clean up these after your departure. But only the black-headed gull breeds in the high hills, selecting (but often changing it in a subsequent season) some pool surrounded by a peat bog or morass where it can build a bulky nest protected from foxes and dogs by water and quagmire. Placed on tufts of molinia or rushes, many nests are often awash, if not afloat, after heavy rain. These nesting colonies, usually below the 2,000 ft contour, are well advertised by the incessant *kwarring* cry, which can be heard far across the open waste. It seems surprising that this gull is able to rear enough posterity to increase as it does, considering the many ground predators which are attracted by the vocal advertisement, including inquisitive egg-collecting humans. In wet summers the nests may all be drowned; in droughty seasons every egg or chick may be taken by predators arriving dry footed.

The bird-watcher exploring the high hills will find other and more common species not described in this chapter, but whose distribution is mentioned in the annotated list (page 203). Wherever there are good stands of heather he will put up red grouse—most numerous on the eastern moors—and hear the loud *go-back, go-back* as they whirr away. Descending to the wooded slopes and dingles he may hear the soft cooing challenge of the black grouse, once almost extinct in Wales. It has made a strong recovery in the present century, particularly where it finds cover in the new forestry plantations. In certain places it is now possible to witness quite substantial 'leks', those very curious spring gatherings of the males (blackcock). With fanned tail and wheezy crowing each cock displays on his little square of territory, awaiting the plain female (greyhen) to select the partner of her momentary choice; usually (it is said) she walks up to the most gorgeous and active exhibitionist. But after one or more matings, the greyhen walks away, and the cock resumes his posturing before other males. The greyhen does all the domestic work of incubation and rearing the family, in which the polygamous cock takes not the slightest interest.

The considerable planting of conifers upon upland slopes and moors which were formerly sheep runs has often been bemoaned by lovers of the bare hills. This planting of non-indigenous trees has changed the fauna and flora considerably, but has not been without interest to the naturalist. Woodcock have increased as a nesting species in this favourable environment of damp upland wooded rides. As the conifers have become seed-bearing they have attracted certain seed-eating finches largely absent in Wales previously. Siskins are breeding regularly, and crossbills have nested several times and may become permanent residents as the yield of spruce, larch and pine cones increases. Even more abundant is the lesser redpoll, which has colonised almost every large conifer plantation in Wales at the stage when the young trees reach about 10 ft in height.

The old indigenous deciduous woods in the deep upland dingles are traditionally the home of two insect-eating summer visitors, both nesting in holes. The common redstart is present in fair numbers, easily recognised, of course, by the bright orange-red tail flicking restlessly. It prefers rather open woodland with old, often half-rotten trees in which it can find a nest-hole; but it freely accepts a nest-box, or a hole in a cottage wall.

Arriving about the same time in April, the pied flycatcher is just as willing to use a nest-box. Foresters who are ornithologically minded have shown that both redstart and pied flycatcher can be attracted to nest in young plantations by a plentiful provision of nest-boxes therein; and of course they are welcome because of their appetite for mosquitoes, horse-flies and other obnoxious insects. Both are delightful birds to watch in the spring, the handsome cocks inviting the attention of the more sober hens to the nest-hole, showing off their bright breasts, black in the redstart, snow-white and dazzling in the flycatcher, and singing their short, simple songs.

Lowland birds

Between the mountains and the sea the land of Wales is rarely smooth. Only around the river estuaries is the country almost level where alluvial soil and sea-washed sand have been reclaimed with earth dyke and drained with ditch; and beyond lie saltings exposed at low tide. This rare flat land is rich in aquatic plant and animal life. There are many water-loving birds, from the large herons, geese, ducks and waders to the tiny warblers.

Three summer visitors to Wales reach their north-westwards limit here in Britain. The yellow wagtail nests only in the water-meadows; and the reed-warbler in the reed-beds, in the border counties, from Flint south to Monmouth and east Glamorgan (but it has occasionally nested in Anglesey). That lover of the lowland copse along river valleys, the nightingale, is confined to such habitats in the last two counties. Rarely it may wander west and north in the spring, sing for a while, but not nest. A sweet bird song heard at night in the rest of Wales will most likely be either that of the woodlark, or the lively mimetic song of that Welsh nightingale—the sedge-warbler.

Hundreds of sedge-warblers pass through the coasts and islands on migration, and pairs remain to sing and nest beside almost any waterside copse or rushy corner with sufficient tall annual vegetation in Wales, breeding at Skokholm, Skomer and Bardsey. Commonly associated with this warbler is the reed-bunting (an increasing species at a time when other buntings seem to be decreasing); the simple stammer of the handsome black-cowled cock can be heard from its song-post near the nesting place, which can be in a great variety of situations, from wind-blown creeping willow on a remote island, to new-planted conifers on damp dunes. Here too you may hear the reeling song of, but seldom see, the skulking grasshopper-warbler, haunting alike the low cover of wet bogs and dry heaths.

Where there are stretches of open water of any size, fringed with reeds, water-lilies, and perhaps alder, typical species are mallard, coot and moorhen; and where the water is deep enough for diving and well supplied with small fish, little and great crested grebes may nest. On the larger lakes look for the nesting shoveler, teal, tufted duck and pochard. As a result of careful watching and listening you may be exceptionally lucky and find some rarer bird nesting—which you would be wise to keep to yourself and some reliable friend until the brood is hatched—such as black-necked grebe, or in the marsh nearby the spotted crake. Both have nested from time to time in Wales.

Herons stalk or stand sentinel by every piece of water, from tiny stream and wet ditch to largest river and lake. They are sparsely distributed but nest in every county save Denbigh and Flint. A BTO census, 1964–7, when many birds were slowly recovering from the losses of the severe winter of 1963, shows that the highest counts of occupied nests for each county were: Anglesey 20, Caernarvon 63, Merioneth 16, Montgomery 2, Cardigan 41, Radnor 10, Brecon 6, Pembroke 18, Carmarthen 53, Glamorgan 27, Monmouth 28. To which must be added at present, perhaps another 10 per cent for overlooked nests and a continuing build up. Welsh heronries are mostly small, under twenty nests as a rule, the largest in trees, the smallest, and single nests, occasionally in cliffs. A round total of 300 nests (from the above census) would mean 600 breeding adults, and possibly 600 non-breeding sub-adults. Not a large total for the whole of Wales, but the heron is freely shot by fishermen and river bailiffs (despite the good it does by living much on that predator of young sporting fish, the eel). Because they are so conspicuous by their large size and ponderous slow flight, they are seen more often, giving rise to a belief that they are very common, which is hardly the truth.

The young herons hatch early in April, and are able to flap out of the nest in June. They wander independently, and in their first autumn travel farther than they do once they have established nesting sites in the succeeding years. In July and early August they often visit the western offshore islands; and in winter they fish the rock pools along the seashore when inland waters are frozen.

Anglesey with its many little lakes and fens may be considered the headquarters of the ducks breeding in Wales: mallard, teal, pochard, shoveler and tufted duck already mentioned, and from time to time rarer species. In winter these waters, which seldom freeze for long in the island's mild climate, are wonderful places for watching large flocks of wigeon, pintail, wild swans and geese, as well as the resident ducks; and if the fresh water does freeze, these water birds join the winter congregations of sea-ducks and waders in the many bays and estuaries hard by. This applies also to a few other large sheets of fresh water near the sea elsewhere, especially in South Wales (Orielton Decoy, Kenfig Pool, Eglwys Nunydd Reservoir), and the estuaries along all coasts.

Feral populations of both the Canada and grey-lag goose are now ranging freely over Anglesey, nesting in certain favoured places. Some are from escaped aviary stocks; others have been deliberately freed, including Canada geese now nesting in Pembrokeshire. Many get shot, for they are less wild than the truly wild geese which annually winter in Wales. The list of wading birds which are seen on the estuaries from autumn to spring is long, and is enumerated in the species list (page 203); it includes some waders which breed both on the fells and along the foreshore and marshes by the sea.

The blue and gold flash of the kingfisher delights the eye on many a more slowly flowing stream, river and clean water of the lowland countryside. The few Welsh canals are also plentifully supplied with minnow and other small fry, and are favourite

feeding haunts; although the canal banks are not too well supplied with steep earth banks overhanging sufficiently for the
kingfisher to excavate its tunnel nest. In winter it wanders far
afield; there is a southward movement along the coast, probably
largely of immature birds, which begins in late summer, and
some leave Wales altogether over the cold months. As
a regular nester it is rather thinly distributed, suffering losses
in severe winters, but returning to inhabit all clean waters
each summer.

Using the same river banks for its tunnel nest, as well as disused
sand and gravel pits, drainage holes in embankments over water,
and occasionally in earth cliffs over the sea, the sand-martin is
most numerous along the main rivers of the Severn, Wye, Usk,
Conway, Clwyd and Dee in Wales. It often arrives in March,
and remains until September. Rogers & Gault (1968) carried out
an excellent survey, part of a general enquiry of the BTO, of the
distribution of the sand-martin on the river Usk, with results
which are doubtless typical of other substantial rivers in Wales.
Ignoring the tributaries they counted 1,850 occupied nest-holes
(=3,700 breeding adults) along the main river Usk between
Aber Camlais and the sea; 73 per cent were classified as well-
defined colonies, the largest of which had 210 occupied holes;
the remainder were loosely defined colonies. Nearly 4,000 sand-
martins were ringed during this valuable field work; recoveries
from these show an expected migration southwards to Europe,
with many recaptures by other ringers working sand-martin
roosts in reed-beds in England.

The house-martin in Wales nests up to a high altitude in the
hills, though rarely above 1,000 ft (probably because there are
few buildings to attach its nest to); and will fix its mud cradle to
the overhang of sea-cliff, and of slate and other quarries. Recently two pairs have nested at Skomer on a low north-facing
cliff over the sea, quite ignoring the wide eaves of the warden's
lodge a few feet above. Most nests are hung under the eaves of
country houses, barns and outbuildings.

Swallows appear earlier than house-martins, often in March,

but rarely begin nesting until late in April. They build their cup nest resting upon beam or rafter or ledge in buildings, from mountain farm to lonely island (as many as five pairs have nested in the same year at Bardsey), the commonest hirundine in Wales. The dashing high-flying swifts although very widespread on migration, from April to June, have a curiously local distribution as breeders in Wales. Nesting in cracks under eaves, they are most plentiful in large villages and small towns, but scarce or absent from many exposed coastal villages. Probably the swift cannot find a sufficient supply of the winged insects in the cool sea winds in the upper air it loves to haunt. Yet it can be seen on this west coast flying strongly out over the open sea towards Ireland at almost any time in the summer, especially late in the day. Some of these may be genuine non-breeding migrants exploring westwards for a future nesting season; but possibly many spend the night high in the air over the sea, and return at dawn. It is now virtually proved that many swifts, which have no duties at the nest, ascend into the sky about sunset, and spend the night on the wing, presumably drifting in a state of half-sleep or catnap, 'resting' and only awake sufficiently to maintain position with flap and glide. The long flight to winter quarters in southern Africa begins as soon as the young are fledged late in July. It is believed that the swift has by then accumulated enough body fat to make it possible to make the 5,000 mile journey with few or no landings; and possibly this scythe-winged master of the air may remain on the wing for most of its non-breeding period of the year. (Certainly it is never or very rarely seen to settle to a roost at that season; the air over the African land is warm—for it is summer there—and rising air currents at night would support the swift in 'winged repose'.)

Two common resident birds, like the swift virtually dependent upon man for nesting sites in town, village and farmhouse, are or were in Wales almost as local as the swift: the starling and the house-sparrow may be scarce or missing in outlying villages and farms. However, they have lately increased even in these remote situations, sparrows especially, where poultry have been kept in greater numbers. They are more numerous in autumn, when in local movements sparrows flock to coast farms to feed on the harvest fields, and may settle for the winter if the food supply continues. Hawks and owls take toll. In the spring the experienced breeders which have survived return to (some never leave) old nest sites where the males, now in handsome glossy plumage and chirping song, call to their mates to renew the partnership. This is the time of year when the young sparrows, born in the previous summer, wander much in search of territory, appearing briefly on remote islands, at lonely farms on coast and mountain, but if, after a day or two of vain chirping, they fail to establish a nest site and mate, they vanish like faint-hearted pioneers.

Tree-sparrows are comparatively rare in Wales. They, too, turn up in spring along the coast, then vanish. There are small breeding colonies in low-lying country along the eastern border, in Anglesey and sporadically elsewhere.

Starlings in Wales may be divided into two distinct populations. First, the residents which perform only local feeding movements, moving down from upland farms and villages in winter, and roosting in certain sites—shrubberies, ivy on old buildings and cliffs, in caves, disused mine shafts, and quarries, which may be used throughout the year except when nesting. And second, a very large winter influx made up of foreign visitors, chiefly from the north and east of the British Isles and Europe. These feed and roost by tens of thousands in the mild lowlands of Wales, in reed-beds and evergreen coverts; and I have seen an immense flock settle to sleep on Ramsey Island in the light of a wintry sunset. Broods of locally born starlings in unspotted plumage first appear on the coast and islands at the end of June; but the foreign invasion does not reach its climax until late autumn.

Two resident doves or pigeons have greatly increased of late years. Fifty years ago the woodpigeon (ringdove) was more or less confined as a breeding bird to well-wooded country, although commonly distributed in winter. Today it can be found building its flimsy nest platform in bush and furze on the sea-cliffs; although most of the eggs or young from these sites may be lost to predatory gulls, jackdaws, crows, ravens and magpies. However, the woodpigeon is a persistent breeder, and will lay eggs from April to October.

The stock-dove, plain dark blue at a distance, with a more rapid dashing flight as if forever fleeing from man and other enemies, has also increased, and now breeds in all counties inland and along the coast, even at Skomer and Skokholm. It rarely associates with rock doves in the same habitat; it is less sociable, does not frequent caves, but places its two eggs well inside a hole in the rocks, or in a rabbit-burrow. Inland it haunts well-timbered country as a rule, resting in holes in trees, old buildings, derelict mine shafts, and crags up to 1,000 ft altitude. Usually you will see the stock-dove in pairs, or very small parties; but look carefully at winter flocks of woodpigeons, for the stock-doves when hungry will feed with these larger doves on acorns, and in the same pastures and crops. I once saw some stock-doves feeding with turnstones amid the seaweed along the tide-line, evidently finding seeds washed ashore with the jetsam, while the turnstones were picking up their crustacean and other animal food.

The pretty collared dove, in the course of its spectacular colonisation of north-west Europe, hardly arrived in Wales before 1960. Yet it has since spread to every county, but erratically, at random. Thus although by 1966 it was nesting in a strong resident colony at St Davids, farthest west village in Wales, it was present but not proved to breed in Glamorgan. A flock of 200 was counted in Anglesey by 1967 at a date when it had not yet been proved to breed in Brecon or Carmarthen. It has not yet reached the state of being, like the house-sparrow, a parasitic pest to poultry- and duck-keepers, as it has in some parts of England.

The migratory turtle-dove, superficially like the collared but without the black neck-band or the conspicuous white half of the undertail, is a lover of bushy, scrubby woods and coverts. In

Wales it is seen everywhere on migration, appearing usually
early in May, and departing in September. Only a few remain to
nest, chiefly in the border counties, notably Monmouth.

The inland woods contain the three leaf-warblers. Most
numerous of course is the sweet-voiced willow-warbler, happy
with low covert and copse, with orchard, tangled hedgerow and
young plantation. The chiffchaff needs a higher singing post
from which to utter its far-carrying double note; it does not
usually ascend so far up the mountainside, but will nest in small
copses tucked away in sea-ravines if these have suitable song-
posts; it will utilise a telegraph pole and even TV aerial within
its summer territory. The largest and least common is the wood-
warbler, arriving late in April, and confined to tall deciduous
woods, especially those on hillsides which also have some undergrowth in which the domed nest can be hidden. Here, amid the
voices of commoner singers, the shivering sibilant whisper of the
wood-warbler can give much pleasure; perhaps because the bird
is first seen while the tall oak, ash and beech trees are full of light
before their leaves have half unrolled, the ground below a sheet
of blue and yellow with bluebells and wild daffodils, the whole
world of nature rich with promise of spring.

The leaf-warblers look alike, but their songs are very distinct.
The reverse is the case with the blackcap and garden-warbler,
both haunting undisciplined rough woods with thick undergrowth. The songs of these summer warblers are very similar,
the blackcap's sharper, more staccato, but if in doubt you must
wait to catch sight of the singer—if he has no black skullcap he
is, of course, the softer-voiced garden-warbler. Although nesting
in much the same cover, the blackcap seems to like the occasional
tall tree; nevertheless the exception proves the rule and I have
watched the garden-warbler singing at dawn, fully exposed on a
bare branch of an unfelled oak towering above the secondary
growth of a forest; this species nests more widely in Wales than
the blackcap, perhaps, ascending fairly high up mountain slopes
to sing and breed in young plantations with thick tangle of
bramble and thorn undergrowth. The garden-warbler never,

Page 107 (above) Young guillemots leave the cliffs when less than three weeks old; (below) storm petrel with egg in a rock crevice (uncovered) at Skokholm

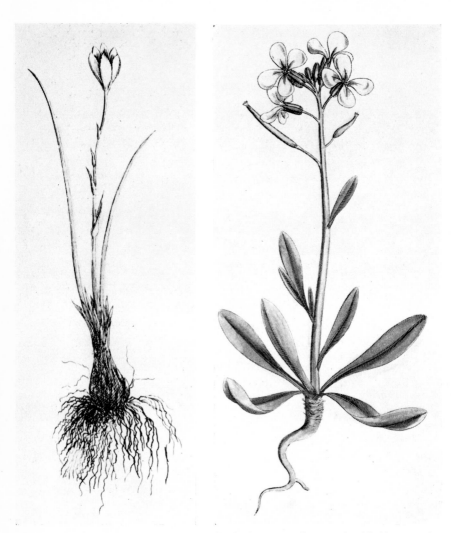

Page 108　Found only in Snowdonia: (*left*) *Lloydia serotina*, the Snowdon lily (from Ray's *Synopsis Methodica*, 1696); (*right*) *Matthiola incana*, a rare sea stock or gillyflower

but the blackcap quite often, winters in woods and shrubberies along the Welsh coast.

Typical of the deciduous woods and the nearby tall hedges is one of the rarest of the tits, or at least one seldom correctly identified. This is the willow-tit, which excavates a nest in rotten timber. Compared with the marsh-tit, which it so closely resembles, the willow has rather a dull sooty black cap, without the gloss of the marsh, but the broad light patch on its wing is more obvious. More positive evidence is the call note of the marsh, a typical *pit-pit-chou*, compared with the almost nasal *chay-chay-chay* of the willow. With practice a keen ear will learn to recognise other soft, less distinctive notes. The distribution of both is still a challenge to observers; but W. M. Condry considers that the willow-tit is more widespread than the marsh-tit, especially inland, in Wales, where it reaches high up to the limit of deciduous woodland and the thickets on the edge of mountain bogs. The marsh-tit never excavates a nest hole, but adopts a natural hole or a nest-box.

In these same upland deciduous woods redstart and pied flycatcher nest (page 98); and in still more open country, but also in young conifer plantations, the tree-pipit is a summer singer, using a taller tree or pole as a watchpost, rising from it periodically to sing its simple aerial song. Here, too, the nightjar used to be quite common, crouching all day in the bracken and heath in open glade or ground litter in lately felled woodland. Thirty years ago you could hear its reeling song and find its neutrally coloured eggs or chicks even on the windswept islands, but there has been an almost catastrophic decline in the numbers breeding in the British Isles, and although still nesting here and there in Wales, chiefly in the southern counties, it is, alas, now almost rare.

Three woodpeckers nest in all counties in Wales: the green and great spotted are thinly distributed everywhere in about equal numbers. The sparrow-sized lesser spotted species is much scarcer: most county avifaunas describe it as 'few and local, but increasing slowly'.

G

From near extinction in the bitter winter of 1963 the wood-lark, perhaps the sweetest voice of all Welsh singing birds, is slowly recovering. Before that year it was more numerous than the skylark in upland farming country where fields are small, often with wind-stunted trees; but it also nested right down to sea-level, occasionally upon open heaths frequented by breeding skylarks. Two pairs nested in a 4 acre walled garden surrounded by woods at Orielton in 1958.

Leaving the shelter of woods for the open heath, the stonechat is a conspicuous bird of the furze-grown wastes close to the sea which one associates with other heath birds—linnet, yellow-hammer, skylark, meadow-pipit, cuckoo, curlew and lapwing. The stonechat used to nest on many inland heaths, but has almost ceased to do so since the cold spell of 1963. You are more likely to see the whinchat far inland and well up the hillside to 1,000 ft, where it is most at home in young plantations, dwarf hedgerows, open country with scattered bushes, and especially boggy stretches with such growth. The handsome cock utilises the tops of bushes and fence posts from which to sing its brief warbling song.

Birds of the coast

Of special interest because of its rarity elsewhere, the charming red-billed, red-legged chough still survives in small numbers in Wales. It can be watched along the rock-bound western coasts, in Snowdonia, and at certain inland cliffs and slate quarries. The last pair in England died recently of old age, in Cornwall. The species has dwindled to a very few pairs in Scotland; and seems to be on the decline, even in its main stronghold of the west of Ireland. A census of 1963 showed that at least 100 pairs were counted in Wales, chiefly in Caernarvonshire (coast and slate quarries) and Pembrokeshire (coast only), although it is still possible that many pairs were overlooked.

Two factors may be helping the chough to hold its own at present in Wales: rabbit gin-traps, in which they were frequently caught before 1955, are now illegal; and the peregrine falcon, which undoubtedly killed a proportion annually, has become much scarcer as a breeding bird in Wales.

The chough usually builds its stick and twig nest in the roof of a cave, in a rock crevice in cliff or quarry, or in a disused mine shaft; most of these sites are inaccessible except by ladder—perhaps another reason for its comparative success in Wales. The cock can be seen assiduously bringing food to the hen; she alone incubates. The quiet observer can study the pair at fairly close quarters as they dig with curved crimson bill for worms, grubs and insects in the short turf which, like starlings, they exploit for food. The pair remain attached for life upon an established territory, which may be a few miles of coast. In Snowdonia choughs have been recorded flying above the highest point, 3,560 ft (it was, I think, Hillary who saw a red-billed chough above him when he reached the summit of Mt Everest, 29,000 ft high); but in Pembrokeshire they rarely fly far inland.

The chough is often mistaken for the jackdaw, and vice versa. Size and voice are similar, but with a little experience the *kyāā* call of the chough can be recognised: it is distinctly higher in pitch, more prolonged and more musical than the clack of the daw. The flight is also different, a series of erratic butterfly-like flaps and glides, with primaries widely splayed. The two species live close together, but have different food spectrums, the daw living much in association with man, exploiting farmyards, arable fields and joining rooks in pasture fields. Large flocks of daws can be seen flying to roost in the cliff haunts of choughs, but it is rare to see more than a dozen choughs together in Wales; at most you might see twenty in the late summer and autumn when two or three family parties join up; and occasionally half a dozen immature choughs may remain together during the summer, sociable but non-breeding.

Of all the birds of the Welsh coast those of the grand colonies of nesting sea birds dominate the thoughts of visiting and resident ornithologist alike. They are most spectacular on certain small islands described elsewhere in this book: Skomer and Skokholm, lonely Grassholm with its huge gannetry, Ramsey with its high cliffs, St Margaret's and Caldey joined at low tide—all in Pembrokeshire; and in North Wales, Bardsey and Puffin Island. Smaller islands, less remarkable but always interesting, include Flatholm, Glamorgan; Middleholm, Pembroke; Cardigan Island, Cardigan; St Tudwal's Islands, Caernarvon; and the Skerries off Anglesey. Other islands are linked by causeways to the mainland, such as Llanddwyn and Holy Island in Anglesey, the latter famous for its South Stack cliff birds.

Those powerful flying machines, the gulls, are everywhere dominant. With the availability of new food supplies in the exposure of man's wastes at rubbish dumps, sewer outfalls, fish wharves, and the fish offal and galley wastes from ships at sea they have vastly increased in numbers. The herring gull is the most numerous; in total many thousands breed along the whole coast where there are cliffs and rocky islands upon which it can build its nest in comparative safety. Occasionally it will nest on flat open ground with other gulls. Once fully mature and established as a breeder it is resident, never travelling very far from its established beat between roosting and feeding areas. These adults have regular feeding routes, keeping to a time-table from the moment of leaving the roost (on cliffs, islands, sea or reservoir) before sunrise, until the hour when they drift back, fully fed, before the sun sets. Small flocks feed along the shore, perhaps flying out to attend any fishing or passenger boat in sight; others scan the countryside for signs of human activity, such as ploughing or cultivating arable ground, in order to glean worms and grubs behind the machines. Some regularly attend car parks and picnic sites for scraps they expect to find or be given: the top of Snowdon is a favourite resort, profitable on any fine day. In the ports and harbours this gull becomes hand tame; and, relying on the goodwill of local workers and residents, will impudently build its nest on the roof of waterside buildings. Although it is a scavenger of all kinds of edible rubbish, including tainted food, it is extremely clean in its attention to its plumage, washing thoroughly after each meal, usually in fresh water, which it will fly some distance to find, even if the sea is nearer.

Less than 100 years ago the great black-backed gull was rare in Wales. Now it is a fast-increasing species. Although far less numerous than the herring gull, it nests on all the principal cliff sites, singly or in small groups, and is master of every other bird save the peregrine falcon. Lordly it looks in its soaring, gliding leisurely flight; but is tough on small birds, their eggs and young. In the summer each great gull will account for several of the smaller sea-birds in each week of living in or near their colonies; in total hundreds of adult puffins and shearwaters are surprised and mauled to death at their burrows; while the huge eggs and chicks of guillemot and razorbill are carried off, the chicks often being swallowed in one gulp. When ringing these nestling auks I used to collect all pellets I could find regurgitated by the great gull, and frequently retrieved from them the undigested legs of auk victims, some with rings still attached.

Young rabbits, unwarily feeding far from their shallow natal burrow, are stalked or swooped upon, or, if they escape, the great gull may dig down to the doe's nest, unless the doe is present and prepared to drive the bird away. I have seen this gull kill an adult rat which was feeding near it at a rubbish dump, with one blow of its leaf-shaped dagger bill; for it is also a scavenger, particularly of carcases of domestic animals, and of dead seal and porpoise washed ashore. Farmers accuse it of plucking out the eyes of cast sheep. Altogether an unpopular gull, which has to be kept down in numbers at the island reserves where it has so greatly increased. In winter it wanders far along the coast and inland, and immatures continue a wandering life throughout the year.

The lesser black-backed gull, recognisable by its (herring gull) size, yellow legs and slate grey, not black, mantle, arrives in March, settling to nest during April, first eggs early in May. By preference it is a colonial nester, with large colonies on Newborough Warren, Puffin Island, Skomer, Skokholm and Flatholm; also breeding along the shore of all coastal counties save those without steep cliffs. Occasionally it has bred inland, as at Cors Tregaron, where like the black-headed gulls, it is to some extent protected by quaking bog.

Interestingly, during the present great expansion of gull numbers, both herring and lesser black-backed species have taken to nesting on roof-tops far inland, but near their source of natural food in the fields as well as scavenging food around the towns. An established colony of some sixty pairs of both these gulls was first reported in May 1958, but apparently had become established some years earlier, nesting on a factory roof at Merthyr Tydfil, and many young were reared. When some thirty-five pairs of each returned next year they were persistently harried because of the mess they had created, and prevented from rearing any young. By 1963 probably the same colony was re-established and rearing young on roofs of a factory estate some 6 miles away at Hirwaun. Other small roof colonies of both these gulls have been reported elsewhere in Wales, but closer to the sea, and some nesting upon 'mothballed' ships laid up in creeks. The majority of lesser black-backs migrate south late in summer and early autumn; a few are seen throughout the winter, and some of these are recorded as having the slate black mantles typical of the more northern breeding race *Larus f. fuscus*.

In some sites in Wales the cliff-nesting kittiwake has increased, but as a strictly oceanic gull it does not benefit from the abundant wastes provided by man ashore. At best it follows fishing boats at sea, but discreetly, for this small dainty-looking gull is at the bottom of the peck order, bullied by the larger sea-birds in the competition for the offal thrown overboard at each haul of net or line. The largest colony in Wales is at Skomer (see page 198), where a census in 1967 showed well over 1,500 pairs. It requires sheer cliff walls, attaching its nest of seaweed, grass and droppings to mere fingerholds of rock, preferably with the open sea below. Thus in Wales it is restricted to the counties of Anglesey, Caernarvon, Pembroke and one colony in Gower.

The graceful sea-swallows or terns are seen regularly on migration along Welsh coasts and often over fresh water, but the

few that remain to breed are dwindling in numbers because of
the continued invasion of their vulnerable ground-nesting sites.
Anglesey seems to be their main refuge in Wales: here still breed
common, arctic, roseate, Sandwich and little terns. There are one
or two sites elsewhere in North Wales, but none in South Wales
at present. A census of the little tern in Wales in 1967 yielded
eight colonies but only thirty-five pairs.

Three auks breed in some numbers in those counties which
have substantial cliffs: Anglesey, Caernarvon, Pembroke and
Glamorgan. The largest concentrations of puffins, guillemots
and razorbills are on Skomer Island (about 12,000, 2,500, and
1,700 pairs respectively). The three penguin-like birds share the
rock-bound shore and cliffs with a nice economy. Smallest in
size, the puffin lays its single white-looking egg well down a
burrow which it digs or takes over from a rabbit; it feeds its
chick on very small raw fishes and sand-eels. The razorbill does
not burrow, but utilises recesses in the cliffs or beneath boulders
and loose stones, even occasionally a short distance inside a rabbit
burrow, where its handsomely marbled and scrolled egg is
reasonably safe from rolling into the sea, as well as less subject to
the attacks of marauding gulls and other birds; it feeds its chick
on much the same raw diet of little fishes carried cross-wise in
the powerful razor bill, and to this extent it seems to be in some
competition for food with the puffin (Peter Corkhill, warden at
Skomer, has seen the razorbill try to rob the puffin of its load of
small fry by hustling it on the sea beneath the breeding cliffs).
Both have thick heavy bills adapted for catching and holding
several small fish at the same time. Curiously too, both puffin
and razorbill have two brood patches, arguing that at one time
both laid two eggs. Also the puffin's egg, superficially white
(like most eggs hidden deep in holes) is not really so: held up to
the light it exhibits a faint zoning of lilac markings at the big end,
suggestive of evolution from a protectively coloured egg formerly laid in the open. We may suppose therefore that the
puffin's burrow-nesting habit has been acquired comparatively
recently in the centuries of the bird's evolution, and that the egg

will tend to become purer white now that it is no longer exposed to the light.

The guillemot is an example of a bird which has survived in its present exposed nesting situation by adaptation in the opposite direction. It lays its huge protectively coloured egg on open narrow ledges, where its pyriform shape reduces the risk of rolling off. It has only one brood spot between the legs—an economy in a species so crowded together that there is standing room only. And it has adopted communal habits of incubation and care of the young (now found to be characteristic of some of the communally nesting antarctic penguins). 'Aunts and uncles' —that is, individuals other than the parents—will brood the egg or feed the chick, and help fence it in from danger of toppling over the edge, and from attack by predators. The guillemot chick is fed on much larger fish than the other auk chicks, so large indeed that only one fish can be fed at a meal; and even so you will see the adult holding that large single fish lengthwise with the tail protruding from its long slender bill for a long time before handing it over. There is a good reason for this delay: the tough bony head of the fish is being softened in the stomach of the adult by powerful digestive juices—a remarkable adaptation for the convenience of the chick's tender digestive system. Finally the guillemot (also the razorbill) chick is extremely precocious, and leaps down to the sea, away from the dangers of the cliffs, when only half grown at from two to three weeks old. Once on the water it is convoyed and protected by one adult for several weeks until it is full grown. The young puffin, however, remains in the perfect safety of its natal burrow for a total period of about seven weeks, becoming mature and fat enough to withstand the fast then imposed upon it, when the parents tire of feeding it and fly away to moult at sea. Presently the deserted 'puffling' makes its own way down to the sea—and wisely at night, when the predatory gulls are asleep.

While the numbers of puffins, razorbills and guillemots continue to decline in Wales, the populations of some of the petrel family, like those of the gulls, have increased substantially. The

auk decline has been put down in part to the increasing menace
of oil pollution at sea from the swelling world tonnage of oil-
carrying ships. More specifically the auks spend most of their
lives swimming and diving (they may be unable to fly over the
period of the wing-moult), and so are more prone to encounter
and become victims of the filthy slicks of waste oil discharged by
these ships; the free-flying petrels and gulls, living largely on the
wing, can spot and avoid oil.

It was my good fortune for a few years to live on Skokholm
and pioneer a study of the then little-known Manx shearwater,
so conveniently nesting in burrows outside my door there. The
colony on Skokholm, protected, and continuously studied by
the ringing method over the last forty years, has since increased
to some 35,000 pairs, some of which have taken over puffin
burrows as the puffins have declined; others have occupied new
ground dug by rabbits in the now unfarmed island fields. At
least double and probably treble that number nest at Skomer,
and there are smaller colonies on Middleholm and Bardsey, with
odd pairs attempting to breed in burrows and holes in mainland
cliffs. Individuals explore the mainland coast and often fly far
inland at night in summer, evidently unestablished maturing
birds close to breeding; and later, when the flight of the fledge-
lings, weak on the wing and deserted by the adults, begins in the
autumn, if this coincides with severe gales many are wrecked
along the shore or blown inland. But those young shearwaters
which get safely to sea perform the astonishing feat of migrating,
quite alone and unguided by the adults, 6,000 or 7,000 miles
across the equator to winter quarters (actually to the southern
summer), along the coasts of south Brazil and the Argentine.
Ringing has shown that individuals can migrate very fast, at a
speed of several hundred miles a day. How pleasant—to spend
life in perpetual summer! But to accomplish such a long migration unguided argues an inbuilt (genetic) knowledge of the
route; and the present theory is that navigation is by an innate
ability to steer by the sun and star-pattern—plus an acute time
sense; that in effect the young bird is born with a brain carrying

a fully programmed computer which tells it what to do and where to go.

Skokholm is also the main metropolis of the storm petrel in the southern half of the British Isles; this charming swallow-sized sea bird is the Mother Carey's Chicken of the mariner. Dainty and fragile in appearance, it is adapted to the roughest conditions at sea. I have seen it perfectly at ease in a Force 9 gale off Rockall, where a storm petrel fluttered and dived in the wake of our trawler, collecting minute scraps of food churned up by the labouring wallowing ship. But unless you stay by night at Skokholm (see page 198) you are unlikely to see a storm petrel on the wing in Wales. A few may be seen offshore, fluttering on feeding movements past headlands of the Irish Sea, and in the Bristol Channel, by day. They return to their nesting crevices well after sunset, and depart before dawn.

The continuing study at Skokholm has shown that there may be at least a thousand pairs of storm petrels nesting, which is double my original estimate of forty years ago. Ringing of several thousands has proved an interesting interchange of younger individuals between Skokholm and some smaller island colonies in Wales and Ireland. Skokholm seems to be 'full house' for these little birds, and it looks as if they were trying to over-flow on to new island sites. Breeding success at Bardsey has, however, been poor because of the number of little owls which prey upon it there.

The fulmar is another successful petrel. It has spread south from the Arctic increasingly as it exploits the enormous new feeding opportunities resulting from more and more motor fish-ing boats disposing hourly of their offal and waste fish, day and night, offshore of the British Isles. From 1930 onwards the fulmar began to settle on Welsh cliffs, but did not lay the first recorded egg until 1948. Now it is rearing its single chick on all cliff-bound parts of the coast, and on most of the islands, although not so abundant as in Scotland, where it may even nest on house roofs. But now that the latest type of trawler and other fishing boats are carrying processing plant for utilising every scrap of waste fish for conversion to protein meal for farmstock, we may see no further increase of this powerful dominant bird, and even perhaps a decline in numbers.

Gannets are often seen close inshore, diving spectacularly as they follow the herring and mackerel shoals. Their only sizeable colony in England and Wales is at Grassholm (page 186), where about 15,000 pairs nest.

Cormorants, still much persecuted by fishing interests, breed in small colonies on Welsh islands and cliffs, occasionally in trees with herons, and there is one colony well inland at Craig yr Aderyn, Merioneth (on a steep crag overlooking alluvial ground, formerly a tidal estuary). Fishermen loathe the sight of cormorants heading inland, for they know they are rivals bound for the rivers and lakes where the trout provide good feeding. It must be admitted that the cormorant is expert at rounding up the fish living in a river pool. On one occasion, while watching dippers on the upper Towy river, I saw the head of a cormorant glide upstream; the bird dived, brought up and swallowed in rapid succession a small trout, an eel, and then another half-pound trout. Afterwards, too satiated to fly far, it flapped to a nearby overhanging branch, where, later that evening, it roosted with other river-fishing cormorants. Ringing of cormorants at the large colony on St Margaret's Island Reserve has shown that the young cormorants travel southwards and westwards in winter, some as far as the Spanish peninsula (where this bird is shot and eaten as a special delicacy).

The shag is much more sedentary, and strictly marine in its distribution. In the early spring the adults, resplendent with their topnot crests and glossy green-black plumage, seek the holes, caves and ledges of cliff-bound coasts and islands in Wales. On the rock Ynys yr Adar off the west coast of Anglesey the shags have been noted to breed in mid-winter, at any time from mid-November to the end of February. If these exceptionally early nests are lost by storm-waves or other causes, the shag will lay again; and eggs may even be incubated late in July. The young shags wander, but not very far; the old birds seem never to stray far from the local rocks where they spend much time in heraldic attitudes, wings spread—some say to dry their pervious plumage; also maybe to aid digestion after a large meal of flounders?

Characteristic resident of the rocky shore, and also nesting on the grassy tops and rocky outcrops of small islands is the bold handsome noisy oystercatcher. This red-billed, red-legged bird is the sentinel of the Welsh shore, its long piping musical call, often in duet or trio, a warning as well as a displacement activity. At one moment it is alert and screaming the alarm; at the next, satisfied that the observer is harmless, it is fast asleep on one leg. On the island sanctuaries it has become remarkably tame, and has parcelled out the rough land surface in territories which have been counted: for example in 1967 there were 73 pairs at Skomer, 49 at Skokholm, 52 at Bardsey. Yet it is sly enough at slipping off the four protectively coloured eggs laid in a neat scrape lined with rabbit-pellets and small stones, and running away unobserved as you approach. In winter huge numbers may congregate on cockle beds and sandflats: up to 15,000 in the Burry estuary. Here 'the oystercatcher war' has been waged for several decades between the local Sea-Fisheries Committee, supported by the Ministry of Fisheries, against naturalists and members of the County Naturalists' Trusts. The former party wish to destroy, the latter to preserve; meanwhile a detached observer might note that the cockle-eating oystercatchers have co-existed with the human cockle-gatherers for several documented centuries without diminishing the considerable annual yield of these molluscs brought home on donkey-back by the hardy men and women of the Penclawdd shore.

Another wader nesting along the shore, but in very small numbers, the ringed plover prefers to make its scrape on a shingle bank with sandy tidal ground below. Occasionally its nest can be found on a rocky cliff-top in Wales, which is a normal habitat in the far north. It freely associates with other waders, and can be distinguished by its liquid melodious *tui* call, its pied head with black collar, and yellow legs, from the somewhat larger turnstone which is also pied about the head but has orange legs, and does not breed in Wales, although it may spend the summer with us in small numbers.

The only thoroughly marine wild duck nesting freely along the Welsh coast is the large exotic-looking shelduck (although recently—it is good to write—one of the sawbilled ducks, the red-breasted merganser, has begun to nest in Anglesey and the Dovey estuary). As a young man farming 6 miles from the Severn estuary in Monmouthshire I was delighted to find shelducks reconnoitring my fields for nest holes in rabbit burrows and under the bases of decayed trees. Here I would find the duck had lined her hidden nest with the tawny down plucked from her breast; she might lay as many as a dozen creamy eggs. She alone incubated, but her drake was always around, looking vividly out of place as he strolled the greensward of tree-bowered fields. At least once a day she came off the eggs and he escorted her on the 6 mile flight to the feeding ground on the Severn foreshore. The beautiful ducklings hatch after four weeks, and are then walked to the sea, an often hazardous journey through a countryside subject to predatory birds, fox, dog and humans. I once held up busy traffic on the main Cardiff–Newport trunk road to let a family party of shelducks walk across (the drake flew anxiously above, the duck stayed with her ducklings); fortunately motorists were co-operative, and amused.

Shelducks breed in small numbers in all suitable habitats of tidal mudflats and marine marsh in Wales, and usually the nest is well hidden in cover away from the water at high tide. The ducklings reach the shore in mid-June. Often small flotillas of these youngsters join to form larger creches, with one or more adults watchfully near. The breeding drakes seem to defend feeding territories well in advance of the family's arrival, and will drive away the non-breeding adults, which have been idling and dabbling in the same zone. But gradually, as the ducklings become independent, this territoriality wanes. Both the adults and the non-breeders now make an astonishing migration, leaving the fast-growing, still flightless youngsters to feed alone.

On fine summer evenings in July these adults will be seen to fly restlessly over the estuary in small or large skeins, circling round until they reach about 2,000 ft. Here the aerial manœuvres are concluded by some birds, evidently not yet ready to migrate, dropping back to the shore, or perhaps all may return; the sky must be clear and the stars emerging for them to navigate before they will depart. From Welsh shores they fly almost due east, which means heading inland; they cross England on a route which takes them direct to the North Sea, to their ancestral moulting grounds on the huge sand flats of the coasts between northern Holland and southern Denmark—the Waddensee at the mouth of the Elbe river. The distance is about 700 miles, and is probably covered non-stop. Aerial photographs have shown immense numbers of shelduck in late summer, flightless and moulting but safe from gunners on these tidal flats and quick-sands treacherous to the human foot. During a visit to this north-western shore of Germany one July I found it was possible to catch glimpses through the telescope of the distant flocks, from lookout posts on the dune islets of Neuwerk and Scharhorn (artificially created by man) far out on the sands of the Elbe. Among them one could spot the bulky forms of common seals, which at that moment were suckling their new-born pups in safety there.

One may speculate that the shelducks first occupied this shal-low alluvial flat rich in food during the annual moult many thousands of years ago when, after the last glacial period, much of the southern North Sea was land, a swamp where the rivers Thames, Rhine, Weser and Elbe joined in a huge delta. With the general rise of sea-level which enisled Britain some 7,000 years ago, the shelducks continued to use the silty edge of the delta as the water crept up over the great plain. At the peak of the moult at least 100,000 shelduck from all parts of northern Europe are gathered here. The shelducks of the north Wales coast are ob-served to make their flight line on fine July evenings along the coast eastwards and then, following the Manchester Ship Canal as their guide at first, they cross England south of the Manchester conurbation.

There is a small concentration of moulting shelduck, above 3,000 birds, in Bridgwater Bay flats, Somerset. It seems probable, although not proved, that some of the breeding shelduck from the estuaries of South Wales join this group, instead of flying across England. The shelducks return in December, and sometimes there are large concentrations in the more extensive estuaries, reaching a maximum of over 550 off Whiteford Burrows, Gower, in January.

Two smaller birds are resident, and migrate little from their habitat of the shore and neighbouring ground. Where there are caves and overhanging ledges, rock doves breed in increasing numbers. However, only a very few show the characters of the genuine 'blue rocks' of the last century—this pure strain is now found only in the remoter parts of Scotland and Ireland. Welsh rock doves today are predominantly a mixed breed resulting from crosses between wild rock doves and the multi-coloured gone-wild domestic homing pigeons. But this is a quite natural return to the wild. It was from the pure wild rock dove that man obtained the progenitors of his present domestic strains, first by exploiting wild doves in their caves by adding shelves to provide additional nesting sites, then breeding them for the table in dovecotes at home. The Normans introduced the columbarium containing hundreds, even above one thousand, nesting niches in one building. There are several well-preserved examples of these tall, usually round, dovecotes in Wales today—as at Orielton—reminders of the medieval lord's right of columbarium, which included free range for his pigeons over the crops of his unfortunate bondsman tenant or serf. From these stocks have been developed the fast-flying racing pigeon of today. Many of these lose their way in bad weather during long-distance races, and of those which do not return to the home lofts, some help to swell the present substantial feral flocks found on almost all suitable sea cliffs in Wales, swamping the few 'true blues'. Probably the increase of these wild and feral rock-nesting doves is also partly due to the relative absence of their ancient enemy, the peregrine falcon, at the present time.

The other resident small bird is the inconspicuous rock pipit, breeding in established territories along every rocky shore and island, but absent from the low sandy and estuarine areas, except in winter when it is widespread, and may feed some distance inland.

The main river estuaries, whether sandy or muddy, are the haunts of hundreds, often thousands of non-breeding birds—waders, ducks, geese, swans, coots, etc, on passage and in winter; a few may summer there as immatures. They are listed in the Index of Welsh Birds, page 203.

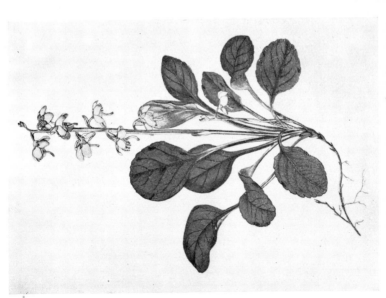

Page 125   Two very rare plants: (*left*) *Pyrola rotundifolia*, found only in Glamorgan and Flint; (*right*) *potentilla rupestris*, found only in Montgomery and Radnor

Page 126 (above) Draba aizoides, the yellow whitlowgrass, found only in Gower, Glamorgan; (below) the very common corn marigold, abundant on light acid cultivated soils

CHAPTER FIVE

Wild flowers

*Variety of floral types – List of Welsh plants –
Collecting – Recording – Lowland plants –
Upland plants – Alpine plants – Flowers of
the coast – Freshwater plants – Fungi*

To THE BOTANIST, amateur and professional alike, the variety of floral types in Wales is satisfying, from the hardy plants typical of the alpine zone of Snowdonia and the Brecon Beacons, to the tender Lusitanian flora of the near frost-free coast. In Wales too there are some stimulating mysteries of distribution in the presence of unexpected, and the absence of expected, plants which, in terms of soil, situation and climate, do not conform to the rules generally accepted by the ecologist.

Then there is always the intriguing problem of the colonising alien, sometimes rare, sometimes vigorously multiplying, but usually rather disdained by the conventional botanist who may prefer the indigenous, the true native. Here research into the literature may be necessary; for the records of the first appearance of certain rare, perhaps exotic, plants, made by botanists long dead, have often been queried, and sometimes finally discredited—only to be honourably rehabilitated in the rediscovery of the plant flourishing in or near the same situation. Plant species can be 'lost' for years, then—like the birds, and sometimes with their help as seed transporters—come back to reinhabit the land and be reinstated on the 'List of living plants'; they may never have been truly absent but rather have blushed unseen by man over the years of official exclusion from the local records. Such a rediscovery is almost as great a joy as the first acquaintance with a 'new' species.

What indeed is a true native? It would be hard to define honestly, although the classifying, collecting instinct of man will insist on labelling as alien those species whose first appearance and spread have been recorded in the literature within, say, the last century. But the amateur field naturalist need not trouble unduly with research into old records. Far more satisfying is the study of the ecology of the living plants which he will encounter; and the 'movement' of species with change of land use is part of that study, part of the fascinating history of survival of local plants vividly enacted year by year.

Mankind has been a considerable and continuing influence upon the local distribution of plants for at least 4,000 years of Welsh history. And indeed earlier, from the moment succeeding waves of immigrants travelled through the newly enisled, heavily forested Britain, carrying seeds of food plants deliberately, and of 'weeds' accidentally (in his clothes, hair, footwear, or mixed with edible grain and food, and in the hair of his domesticated animals). The process still goes on: it is said that modern much-travelled man has accidentally introduced more alien species, in the form of seeds transported in the turn-ups of his trousers and in cars and other vehicles, than all he has ever deliberately imported for planting. There are a few botanists who take the extreme view that any species, no matter how newly discovered, arrived or transported, which can survive and multiply in the local soil and climate, becomes automatically, and therefore deserves to be called, a native.

As the people of Wales rapidly increased in numbers in the early centuries AD, their deliberate destruction of the primeval forest by axe and fire created great changes in the floral landscape. The predominantly woodland scene, rich in ferns but poor in colourful plants, altered largely to a treeless pastoral one, vivid perhaps principally in spring with low-growing flowers and thorny shrubs resistant to grazing. With the plough came several new species which thrive and multiply in arable ground. As the land was settled with permanent homes and farms, enclosures with walls and hedges gave limited sanctuary to certain species surviving from the vanished forest. Today these same hedgerows are receding with modern extensive methods of farming which tend to create almost prairie conditions, with chemical control of unprofitable wild plants. But in the present century there has been some return of forest, largely by the planting of profitable coniferous woodlands on second-class (that is, steep or elevated) land and the poorer soils, especially dunes. Many immemorial stands of slow-growing native oak, beech, ash and other deciduous trees clothing the steep inland cwm have been replaced with quick-growing spruce, larch and fir planted in regimented rows; these conifers gradually impoverish the flora by excluding light, leaving mosses and fungi but few flowers to exist in their shadow.

Fortunately the Forestry Commission, principal owner of conifer forests in Wales, has more recently adopted a policy of planting deciduous, and mixed deciduous-coniferous woodlands, which in future will break some of the drab uniformity of earlier conifer monoculture. Also a growing number of remnants of typical native Welsh deciduous woods have been and are being preserved as nature reserves (listed and described on pages 175–201).

One irreversible development has altered the flora along many linear miles of Welsh country: the widening and straightening of main and secondary roads to cope with the ever-increasing volume of motor traffic and man's passion to travel faster (it is hardly relevant to our discussion here that these new straightened roads have the highest fatal accident rate). The plant life along the verges of these new fast roads is quite debased by the frequent mechanical cutting which produces a smooth lawn of monotonous grass. Worse still is the practice of spraying with weed-killer which produces a nasty brown mess. Naturalists vigorously object to this bourgeois conception of the modern wayside, and insist—without much success—upon less cutting and no spraying, so that more interesting wild plants should be allowed to survive and colonise. Personally I am in sympathy with the new wild flower propagation societies which are endeavouring to reseed ill-treated verges with handsome native flowers; and although some ecologists regard this as unnatural interference with the natural process, in my opinion man needs to repair as quickly and as far as possible this degradation of the wild environment.

Wales still has many delightful winding third-class roads and narrow lanes which for various reasons, such as low traffic and high cost of 'improvement', have been unaltered for many decades; and long may they so remain. They have become refuges for wildlife of all kinds, where speed is impossible and fatal accidents therefore rare. Wisely, too, some naturalists' trusts in Wales have agreed with local road authorities on the creation of nature reserves on certain roadside verges where interesting wild plants need special protection, which includes restriction of cutting until flowering and seeding are completed.

List of Welsh plants

As new species, to say nothing of baffling subspecies, races and clines, are constantly being added to, and some subsequently removed from, the list of flowering plants in every country and region, it is safer here perhaps not to give more than approximate figures for Wales.

The National Museum of Wales records some 1,350 flowering plants for Wales out of some 2,000 species on the list for the whole of the British Isles. Even these round figures are somewhat arbitrary; 'splitters' among botanists make many more, 'lumpers' make the figure less. Of the total for Wales 1,060 are classed as natives, 40 doubtfully native, and 250 introduced or naturalised. This excludes any adventives, species which depend for their survival on continual reintroduction from without. It also excludes the ferns, bryophytes (mosses and liverworts), and other flowerless members of the vegetable kingdom.

Welsh Flowering Plants, by H. A. Hyde and A. E. Wade, pub-

lished by the National Museum of Wales and periodically re-
vised, is an essential guide for those who would check local
records in Wales. In this book the scientific name of each species
is followed by the common English name, then its usual habitat
(woods, hedges, marshes, waste places, alpine, maritime, etc),
and finally the counties in which each species has been recorded.
There is also a useful survey of the geography of the plants of
each of the thirteen counties, with mention of the rarer plants
therein, and of their ecology and distribution pattern due to
geological and topographical features. The large county of Glamorgan tops the list with some 1,150 species recorded; the small
county of Radnor, with little limestone and no coast (perhaps
also less explored), is lowest with 680 species.

The same authors and publishers are responsible for a com-
panion handbook, *Welsh Ferns*, which covers *all* the forty-three
ferns native to the British Isles whether occurring in Wales or
not. With its sub-Atlantic climate and mountainous terrain
Wales is richer in species and numbers of ferns than any part of
England. This excellent guide gives the beginner a sample life-
history, illustrated, of a typical fern (the Male Fern); and there is
an illustrated key to the identification of the species.

Wales is also rich in lichens, liverworts and fungi. Advice on
identifying any of the hundreds of species can be sought by
application to the Department of Botany, National Museum of
Wales, Cardiff. These interesting, often minute, plants are the
province of the dedicated novice and expert, and require much
patience and the use of a microscope.

Welsh trees are described in some detail in H. A. Hyde's *Welsh
Timber Trees* (National Museum of Wales). But in addition to
these guides to the whole of Wales, several county lists have been
published within the last quarter century, bringing up to date the
present distribution (see Bibliography, page 219). It must be
admitted, however, that the traditional practice of showing plant
distribution on county maps is artificial: plants respect no man-
made political boundaries, and it is more satisfactory to plot the
local range of rarer species on the geological map, which also

shows contours—and this should be the aim of every serious student of plant geography.

Recognising this, the Botanical Society of the British Isles adopted a 'Distribution Maps Scheme', using as its unit the smaller, easily identified 10 × 10 kilometre square of the Ordnance Survey National Grid map. Under the scheme observers record the distribution of a plant accurately within each unit simply by giving the letters and figures of the grid reference, in the usual way of site-location. Data for plants throughout the British Isles are thus gradually accumulated, for use both now and in the future. By confining each record to its 10 × 10 km square reference (eg SN 22) and not pinpointing each site with its full 100 metre reference (eg SN 045038 = Carew Castle, Pembrokeshire), the precise whereabouts of rare or very rare species deserving special protection need not be shown.

Collecting

Whether you make a survey of your home 10 × 10 km square, or range much farther afield in compiling your plant list, or both, the work can be exciting and rewarding, provided your identification is correct. To secure this evidence means collecting, examining and recording each species; which is usually done against a key provided by one or other of the modern field guides (page 219). These remarks may seem very elementary to the expert, but as Wales has many interesting and scarce, and some very rare, plants, a few sentences about collecting may inform the visiting amateur, and perhaps act as a warning to the too-acquisitive collector. The latter term refers chiefly to the elderly survivors from the bad old days of keeping the personal herbarium. Fortunately the practice is dying out: herbaria are now largely the province of museums and other institutions of public access. In any case the keeping of the private herbarium involved time, patience and storage space not usually available nowadays. While it satisfied the acquisitive instinct in man it did not teach people botany as effectively as observing the living plant in the field or laboratory, in the way young people are taught to do today.

The equipment, however, is much the same: notebook, ball-point (better than pencil), sharp knife, hand lens and—in place of the metal vasculum—polythene bags. These bags are virtually weightless, keep the plants fresher, and discourage the collecting of large specimens.

Collecting of common species is harmless enough—and one cannot learn botany without it. With less common plants one must use restraint. In certain circumstances even a fairly rare plant might be collected if there is plenty of it in the locality and it is known that no one else is collecting there; if it is a perennial; or if a specimen is wanted for a serious attempt to learn its characters. Conversely even a fairly common plant should be left alone if there is not much of it, if there is a large party with you, or if the plant is an orchid or scarce annual dependent on seed for survival. Another strict rule is never to collect even fairly common plants in botanically famous sites, where pressure from botanists is so much greater and the concentration of species is often of as much interest as the occurrence of rarities. Exciting as the extreme rarities are, to collect them without a very sound reason and merely to satisfy lust to possess is a crime against our fellow naturalists and children; yet all too often in Wales I have met people digging up a rare plant with spade or trowel. In these instances I have sometimes been able to force them to replant; at least in those counties which have local bylaws forbidding uprooting of wild plants.

All this should not discourage the bona-fide student. Where such bylaws exist (as they do now in most counties of Wales), he should acquaint himself with them, and if necessary get the permission of the local council to collect whole specimens (although some council officers might be surprised to be asked!), and thus get to work with a clear conscience. But best of all, if the passion to collect is overwhelming—sketch, paint or photograph the plant where it stands, unharmed.

Recording

The general nature calendar which I began as a boy living in the
river valley dividing the counties of Glamorgan and Monmouth
proved to be unexpectedly useful in recalling accurately the
phenological sequence of the wild flowers. My farm was in a
sheltered corner of Wales, with a flora close to that of warmer
English shires. Entries for early spring mingle pleasantly the
records of flowers and bird song:

> Jan. 16. Chaffinch completes full song (very early). Snowdrops make
> a display, with monkshood shooting, by the river bank. First primrose
> out. Lesser celandine opening. Barren strawberry, greater furze in
> full flower, etc.

The trained student will recognise in this youthful calendar his
own loose-leaf field notebook, from which, in moments of
leisure at home, he transfers data to his card index file. In such an
index each species has its separate card on which dates of flowering, fruiting, distribution, etc, are recorded, with cross references
to collected specimens and authorities consulted.

Lowland plants

Much of Monmouthshire is typical of the Welsh–English border
all the way between the Wye and the Dee rivers. Below the
chain of western mountains the Welsh Marches are beautiful
with rolling hills and long-settled prosperous farmland; and, on
the steeper slopes, woodlands, some new-planted, others still
primitive, immemorial. Depending on the mildness of the
winter, the southern (Monmouthshire) border yields the first
flowers of spring from December onwards, sometimes earlier,
long before the inland border counties. The greater furze *Ulex
europaeus* begins flowering even in September; winter heliotrope
Petasites fragrans, a naturalised garden escape, follows in November, with its broad leaves and sweet vanilla scent; and in late
winter, the conscientious gardener can have a trying time with

the many 'weeds' in a warm Monmouthshire garden—these may continue to flower non-stop from the summer: groundsel, chick-weeds, speedwells and many others.

Woodlands on the steepest slopes have remained pristine because the land was uncultivable. The plant-hunter turns to these ancient deciduous woods in the expectation of meeting the original flora, which he knows will vary with the soil, be it acid, calcareous, heavy, light, or mixed. Some plants tolerate both acidity and base-rich lime soils. The native pedunculate oak *Quercus robur*, with sessile leaves, is characteristic of stiff loam and clay soil; and, with hazel, dominates both lowland and upland woods. As oak is late in leafing, often not until late May, the ground below supports a rich variety of spring flowers—primroses, lesser celandines, anemones, the tiny barren strawberry; and soon the bluebells dominate with their glossy green leaves and rich purple-blue racemes shooting towards the light on brittle stems. It is fortunate that the bluebell can stand a reasonable amount of the heavy picking it suffers from townspeople who invade the woods at this time. So long as the leaves are left in good condition the bulb, like that of the snowdrop and the daffodil, survives well, even increases in size if the flower is cut off or pulled out to its white stem base. Moreover, the bulb is harder to dig up than the shallow root of the primrose, which helps to explain why the latter soon disappears from roadsides near developing towns.

Bluebells thrive almost anywhere, provided the climate is moist and the soil well drained. In Wales they often spectacularly cover acres of completely treeless cliff and island plateau, but only in association with bracken or other deciduous growth which later provides the shade necessary to enable the bulb to mature in moist earth. Similarly, primroses grow on steep moist island cliffs as well as they do in woods and hedgerows if they have some shade for part of the day.

Ash *Fraxinus excelsior* is a tree of lime-rich soil, but it flourishes well on some acid soils near streams. It is very common throughout Wales either in pure stands or mingling with beech and hazel. Often the ground layer beneath is smothered with the dull but determined dog's mercury *Mercurialis perennis*, which likes just so much shade and no more—for which reason it thrives under almost every old-established deciduous hedgerow.

More erratic, more lime-loving, is the cowslip *Primula veris*, found sparingly in Wales in pastures and on banks, where it often overlaps with the primrose. Cross-fertilisation results in plants of striking beauty resembling the true oxlip *P. elatior* (confined to eastern England). This hybrid, which is known as the false oxlip, can be found in many damp and shady places: it has the ball-like umbel of the cowslip but each flower is almost as large as a primrose.

Daffodils and narcissi often run wild out of gardens into woods and upon sandy islands. The truly wild daffodil *Narcissus pseudo-narcissus* resembles some of the cultivated varieties, having a trumpet usually only slightly more yellow than the outer perianth or collar; evidently it must have invaded Wales chiefly from the east, for it is numerous in border counties, where it covers some lowland meadows in such profusion that farmers may charge fees for entry to pick them. But there is in Pembrokeshire what is said by some to be a truly native daffodil, *N. obvallaris*, in which the whole flower is the same bright yellow; it is rather scarce and does not transplant easily.

Other plants which bloom before the oak, hazel, beech and ash shadow the ground include the wild arum *Arum maculatum*, also known as lords-and-ladies and cuckoo-pint. I have found the rare and handsome *A. italicum* in Pembrokeshire woods; it has large green leaves with pale, almost white, midribs and an orange-yellow spadix. The common white *Anemone nemorosa* is abundant in Wales, not only in woods before the leaves shut out the sun, but freely along shady hedge-bottoms. The pretty long-petalled blue *A. apennina* has escaped from some gardens and is quite capable of spreading in a wild state.

By the end of April the number of lowland plants in flower which you may record in Wales should reach well over a hundred, not counting the many burgeoning annual 'weeds' of arable ground which have escaped the hoes and harrow and the all-too-often applied herbicides of gardener and farmer. The complete list is too long to be attempted here, but there are some useful general remarks which can be made on dominant species.

In the rougher pastures innocent of fertiliser-cum-weed-killer, vast sheets of buttercup *Ranunculus* make the meadows golden—chiefly the bulbous species *R. bulbosus* on the drier ground, and the meadow buttercup *R. acris* and the creeping *R. repens* dominating the ill-drained part. The curiously irregular-flowered goldilocks *R. auricomus* is much rarer and confined in Wales to woods on limestone; in some clumps its flowers lack petals, in others they are only half-developed. *Aconitum anglicum* or monkshood loves shady ground; not common, it is a delightful surprise to find its purple-hooded spikes in some damp Welsh woods. Columbine *Aquilegia vulgaris* thrives best on lime-sufficient soils and is found in hedgerows and woodlands, often where beech is dominant. The same can be said for the early purple orchid *Orchis mascula*, present on limestone and boulder-clay soils, but generally rare in much of central Wales, including Merioneth. However, I have seen the dwarf purple orchid *O. purpurella* in coastal marshes in Merioneth. At least thirty valid species of the Orchidaceae are recorded for Wales.

Upland flowers

As spring advances into summer, overwhelming the sheltered lowland vales with a wealth of plants and bosky growth, the higher ground grows ever more attractive. Moorland changes from brown to green, as hardy perennial grasses shoot forth between gorse and heather, and the bracken fronds begin to uncurl. Fine-leaved sheep's fescue grass covers the drier slopes; bents, mat-grass and molinia (moor-grass) dominate the damper more level moor. By June the quaking bog is growing white with the handsome cotton grass *Eriophorum*.

Looking closely at the ground between the heather *Calluna*, bell heather *Erica cinerea*, and bog heath *E. tetralix*, and along the little sheep paths, you find a number of diminutive flowers: typically the heath bedstraw *Galium saxatile*, tormentil *Potentilla erecta* with four yellow petals, distinct from the five-petalled creeping cinquefoil *P. reptans* and the silvery-leaved *P. anserina*; the pretty blue, purple or variegated heath milkwort *Polygala serpyllifolia*; lesser skullcap *Scutellaria minor*; eyebright *Euphrasia officinalis*, which has at least a dozen distinct varieties or segregates in Wales; several kinds of violet *Viola*, including possibly the scarce heath or Smith's *V. lactea*. Lousewort *Pedicularis sylvatica* shows its red spikes in damp places; it can be found at sea-level and up to 2,000 ft. The tiny flowers of pearlwort *Sagina* are everywhere; although most of the species like a salty coastal air, and are abundant on cliff heaths and sandy wastes. *S. procumbens* is the hardy upland species, and has been split into subspecies confusing to the beginner, who will need his hand lens to try to distinguish these varieties—it can consume hours of interesting but often inconclusive study! *S. apetala* is an annual largely confined to limestone and railway-ballast habitats in Wales.

The moorland is conditioned by the intensity of sheep-grazing, and sheep can be more omnivorous than rabbits as regards plant species eaten. In fact the enclosed upland meadow, warren or moor grazed solely by rabbit and hare is often a splendid sight floristically in summer, with primroses, bluebells, foxgloves, skullcap, and the sweet-scented lady's bedstraw, burnet rose and wild thyme.

The peat bogs provide a whole world of fascinating flowers: sundews abound—the round-leaved *Drosera rotundifolia* is commonest; the long-leaved *D. intermedia* is more local, but can be found by careful searching. Both spread their reddish rosettes daisy-wise to claim a few inches of ground on which the leaves lie open, their sticky hairs ready to trap, enfold and digest the unwary flying insect or crawling grub. The great sundew *D. anglica* is extremely local in Wales, but can be seen in Borth Bog; it is often almost afloat in sphagnum, along with the round-leaved species. Here too thrives the lovely bog asphodel *Narthecium ossifragum*.

The large-flowered gorse *Ulex europaeus* which blazes yellow in spring on the coast is replaced on the cool upland by the dwarf autumn-flowering *U. gallii*, with deeper-coloured flowers. It often grows amid stones and rocks and on dry banks where you may find the graceful harebell *Campanula rotundifolia*, as well as a very different looking, yet also vivid blue, member of the *Campanulaceae*, the sheep's-bit *Jasione montana*. Both plants can be found down to sea-level, also in dunes and on sea-cliffs. Other bellflowers are scarce in Wales, but the clustered species *C. glomerata* handsomely adorns limestone and old lime-mortared walls. The ivy-leaved bellflower *Wahlenbergia hederacea* is a much-looked-for prize, a fine slender plant trailing over damp peaty ground, especially in Welsh coastal uplands. Here, not too far from the sea, the (oceanic southern type) bog pimpernel *Anagallis tenella* delights the eye with its tiny flush-pink cups in tight groups on hard-grazed marshy places, alike in neglected upland meadows and on remote island pastures.

Welsh country people regularly collect the mild-tasting purple bilberry *Vaccinium myrtilus*—sometimes known as whinberry in Wales—which begins to ripen late in July. It is really a low-growing deciduous shrub, thriving best on upland slopes; but on the tops of the mountains (Snowdonia and the Brecon Beacons National Parks) it is replaced by the red-berried *V. vitis-idaea*, a tough evergreen known as cowberry.

Alpine plants

Purists say that the definition 'alpine' should be limited to plants of the European Alps, and that some of our high-mountain plants common in the Arctic but absent from the Alps should not be called alpine. But 'high-mountain' has come to mean 'alpine' in layman's language, and for our purpose here it suffices to classify as alpine the plants of the higher mountain tops and crags, rather than divide these into Arctic-Alpine (30 species recorded in Wales), Alpine (10 species), Arctic-Subarctic (4 species), Northern Montane (11 species)—see

Welsh Flowering Plants for a detailed discussion on geographical components.

June is the best month to begin looking for Welsh alpines, for exploring the windy rocks and screes above the sheep-bitten fescue, mat and bent grasses. Of course mountainous Snowdonia, with thirteen peaks above 3,000 ft, has more of the truly alpine plants, but the Brecon Beacons (including the Carmarthenshire Van) up to 2,906 ft, Cader Idris 2,927 ft, Aran Fawddwy 2,970 ft, and the Rhinogs 2,475 ft have their share.

The heights above Cwm Idwal, forming part of the nature reserve of that name in Snowdonia, are well known to botanists, almost too well known, with certain plants surviving from the end of the last Ice Age. The wet windy crags support the least willow *Salix herbacea* and numerous mosses, clubmosses and ferns. On rock ledges between 1,500 and 2,500 ft look for the rare Snowdon lily *Lloydia serotina*, found nowhere else in the British Isles; the Devil's Kitchen is the best-known site, but it also grows on the Glyders and Carneddau groups. *Cardaminopsis petraea* is an arctic rockcress which prefers calcareous rocks and in Wales is confined to Snowdonia (this includes a site in Merioneth). The handsome purple *Saxifraga oppositifolia* is fairly common, even at lower elevations, and so is the mossy *S. hypnoides*; but the arctic *S. nivalis* is rare and survives only on wet Snowdon rocks, where you will also find the dense cushions of the tufted *S. caespitosa*.

The mountain avens *Dryas octopelia* is reported near the Nant Ffrancon Pass, but is hard to find; other rare plants are the holly fern *Polystichum lonchitis*; the alpine hawkweed *Hieracium holosericeum*; the two Woodsias *W. alpina* and *W. ilvensis*; the chickweeds *Cerastium alpinum* and *C. edmonstonii*; the whitlow grass *Draba incana*, and the hair sedge *Carex capillaris*.

Common to the higher rocks and crags of all mountains above 2,000 ft, and often at much lower elevations, typical Welsh alpines include least willow, already mentioned; roseroot *Sedum rosea*; the parsley fern *Cryotogramma crispa*, and several of the spleenworts.

Once again this list of alpine plants is merely a small selection, for lack of space; but it is not complete without mention of a certain shrub species of *Sorbus* (mountain ash and whitebeam family) which although mountain rather than 'alpine' are unique to the Brecon Beacons (described on page 173) limestone. These are *S. leyana*, *S. minima* and *S. leptophylla*, endemic species best seen in the crags of the nature reserves of Craig y Ciliau and Cwm Clydach. As there are at least twenty species of *Sorbus* in the British Isles (including ten species in Wales) there is quite a problem of identification. Fortunately the deepness of toothing and lobing, and the colour, of the leaves in the three rarer species are fairly distinctive. *S. eminens* is a small tree with round toothed leaves so far found only in the Wye Valley limestone woods, and the Avon Gorge.

Flowers of the coast

With a considerable and variable coast, several hundred miles long if measured in and out of every estuary, creek, bay and island, Wales is rich in maritime species. As the climate at sea-level is very mild, with little frost, certain southern-oceanic or Lusitanian species occur, notably in the south-west and Anglesey.

A particularly vivid pattern is to be found displayed on the exposed, principally precipitous cliff-bound coast of Pembroke-shire, between late March and August. While the periodic salt gales inhibit the early growth of tall plants, and retard the appearance of tougher species in the spring, at the same time because of the mild air many flowers appear in sheltered sites weeks earlier than at more inland localities. Thus we have the curious situation in March of rich green grass starred with primroses, lesser celandines, anemones, violets and scurvy grass in sheltered lanes beneath cliffs where all is still withered and brown. But by the end of April the steep exposed salt-washed slopes have responded to the sun and are bright with thrift *Armeria*, vernal squill *Scilla verna*, and violets, soon to be followed by sea campion *Silene maritima* and red campion *S. dioica*. The last may take the stout northern form found in Orkney and Shetland; on north-facing cliffs it may grow with thick densely hairy stems and large flowers—these plants have been enriched with the nitrogen and phosphate from the droppings of sea-birds. On Skomer Island it hybridises with white campion *S. alba* to produce a pale pink variety.

Three vivid yellow flowers are common on western Welsh cliffs: great furze, of course; ladies' fingers or kidney vetch *Anthyllis vulneraria*; and bird's-foot trefoil *Lotus* spp. All these plants seem to have more richly hued yellow flowers close to the sea. To these can be added a somewhat rarer vivid golden flower, that of the prostrate broom *Sarothamnus scoparius* subspecies *maritimus*, as far as I know found only in Pembrokeshire in Wales; it differs from the upright broom in having brighter flowers, densely silken leaves, and by resisting the wind by lying absolutely flat against the ground contours (thus overpowering neighbour plants)—a strikingly adapted and beautiful plant.

The mayweeds, *Anthemis* and *Tripleurospermum*, some scented, others scentless, have maritime types, often puzzling in their variety. These are common on the coast, rooted in scant soil and debris amid broken rock. The common or rock samphire *Crithmum maritimum* is an umbellifer; the golden samphire *Inula crithmoides* is one of the Compositae; both have fleshy leaves resistant to drought in their windy cliff habitat, where they may grow side by side. The leaves of the former can be used to make a pickle. In parts of the south-west the very fleshy Hottentot fig *Carpobrotus edulis* has long been introduced (or its seeds may have been washed up or brought by birds from the Isles of Scilly where it is abundant), and occasionally covers south-facing slopes with its aggressive trailing greenery and magenta or yellow flowers; but a cold winter can almost exterminate it.

Where no rabbit can reach it the handsome tree mallow *Lavatera arborea* may grow as tall as a man, especially on limestone cliffs in the sun. Here too the sea lavenders *Limonium* are interesting, if a little tricky for the beginner; some inhabit rocky

Page 143 (*above*) Four rare Welsh insects:
bee beetle, conformist moth, Ashworths'
rustic, mazarine blue butterfly; (*left*) *chryso-
mela cerealis*, the Snowdon beetle; (*below*)
the Gwyniad, a whitefish unique to Bala
Lake

Page 144 (*above*) Orielton Manor, now a Field Study Centre; a flock of Soay (Viking) sheep from the West Wales Naturalists' Trust island sanctuaries are in the foreground; (*below*) Llyn y Fan Fach, in the Black Mountain, Carmarthenshire

cliffs, others salt marshes; and two are very special. These are *L. transwallianum* and *L. paradoxum*, found respectively only on limestone cliffs in south, and on basic igneous rocks in north, Pembrokeshire. Yellow whitlow grass *Draba aizoides* is another rare limestone lover, found only in Gower.

Another rare plant, confined to one seaside habitat which cannot be named here more precisely than to echo the note in the *Flora of the British Isles* ('Grassy cliffs near Newport, Pembs.') is the perennial centaury *Centaurium portense*. It has large pink flowers on single stems (unlike the smaller clustered blossoms of the common annual *C. erythraea*) and is only found elsewhere (doubtfully in Cornwall) in Brittany and the Atlantic coasts of Spain and Portugal.

In shady nooks in the cliffs grows livelong or orpine *Sedum telephium*; but another sedum, English stonecrop *S. anglicum*, thrives best on dry sunny rocks and wind-dried turf. Wall pennywort or navelwort *Umbilicus rupestris*, closely related to the sedums, is abundant on all acid rocks and walls in Wales, where its fleshy leaves absorb the moisture of sea-winds.

Sea plantain *Plantago maritima* has long narrow leaves, and occurs alike on cliff and salt marsh and by mountain streams. But the buck's-horn plantain *P. coronopus* is extraordinarily variable in form: it can be a minute down-trodden plant on a cliff path, or a huge fern-like specimen hanging from a rock ledge. Seed from these varieties will breed true to its parent stock. *Matthiola incana* is a rare species of stock or gilliflower, found only on the south coasts of England and Wales.

Four maritime progenitors of common vegetables are native on Welsh shores: wild cabbage *Brassica oleracea*; wild radish *Raphanus raphanistrum*; wild carrot *Daucus gummifer*; and sea beet *Beta vulgaris* subspecies *maritima*. Close relatives of the beet are the many oraches *Atriplex*, some of which, with the allied salt-wort *Salsola kali*, are maritime and can flourish together in the gritty debris of cliff gulleys and bird-haunted ledges among the nitrogen-loving chickweeds. The same species grow even more freely along the level shore, around and above the jetsam of the tide line. Like many maritime plants they are succulent, able to store up water against desiccation by salt wind and sun.

Saltwort with its spine-tipped leaves; sea purslane *Halimione portulacoides*, grey and mealy looking; glasswort *Salicornia*; the annual seablite *Suaeda maritima*—these are all rather dull-looking plants which may be covered at high spring tides in salt marshes, and frequently become coated with a deposit of mud as a result. In addition they are difficult to preserve for examination later because of their fleshy leaves, as I have found when trying to identify the numerous varieties which botanists have named. But in these marshes it is easy to recognise the handsome sea aster *Aster tripolium* (which will also grow on cliffs occasionally, especially limestone) making a show with the taller sea lavenders.

Cordgrass *Spartina townsendii* is a vigorous new species in Britain, derived from a cross between two unaggressive cord-grasses, the native *S. maritima*, and *S. alterniflora* introduced from America. Unfortunately the hybrid has begun to dominate tidal flats in parts of Wales to the exclusion of several more interesting plants, so botanists dislike it, and even farmers (who find that it is a useful mud-binder in the early stages of reclamation of silted estuaries) have discovered that it crowds out the palatable native grasses of saltings grazed by their sheep and cattle.

Below normal low-water mark grow the string-like grass-wracks, the *Zostera* or eel-grass, which has declined in the years of the increase of spartina. However, there is no connection of cause and effect here, for *Zostera marina* is not truly an estuarine plant, preferring totally saline conditions and growing under water on a sandy bottom. Roofs may be thatched with a 2 ft thick padding of zostera, the fine leaves of which can be 6 ft or more long, and it is said to last very much longer than straw or reed thatch. It is the favourite food of some wild geese and ducks in autumn and winter. In late summer it used to be so thick and dense in the Channel Islands as to trap and occasionally drown a weak swimmer. The dwarf species *Z. nana* is much rarer in Wales.

Leaving the shore for the sand dunes hard by, you find a

fascinating world of plants adapted to the unstable conditions of moving sand, and among them some handsome flowers. Sea holly *Eryngium maritimum* looks like a pretty kind of thistle, but is really an umbellifer; its defence against shifting sand is to put down deep roots in case of blowing, and to send up its spikes very rapidly in case of accretion, of the sand. The pink trumpet flowers of the sea bindweed *Calystegia soldanella*, on the other hand, lie prone on the sand, produced numerously on rhizomes which creep under the surface and help to hold and stabilise the dune. Here you will be sure to see the yellow horned poppy *Glaucium flavum*, which also grows freely in shingle along the coast—not to be confused with the yellow Welsh poppy *Meconopsis cambrica*, which has a very different habitat and is not confined to the coast, but grows in damp shady places, often high up on mountain crags.

There are several spurges *Euphorbia* inhabiting dune and foreshore, and they can be puzzling, for some are local and rare. Sea spurge *E. paralias* thrives even in mobile dunes. Purple spurge *E. peplis* is so rare that anyone finding it should not collect—it is a tender Mediterranean species. Portland spurge *E. portlandica* is another western species to look for in dunes, and found in every Welsh county.

Freshwater plants

Many of the plants we associate with the mountain bogs (page 138) can be discovered beside lowland lake, pond, river and stream—even by tiny rivulets close to the sea. I have found the insectivorous butterwort *Pinguicula* pressing its rosette of pale green leaves in a trickle of water running into the harbour on remote windswept Skokholm, a suboceanic island. It could have been the rare *P. lusitanica*, found in Wales only in Pembroke, but unfortunately I did not examine it sufficiently at the time, unaware of the likelihood of it being other than the common species *P. vulgaris*, which is abundant on the highest Welsh mountain bogs, and which can also be found in dune slacks close to the sea. Of the bladderworts the lesser, *Utricularia minor*, grows locally in Wales. A northern continental species found from Iceland to north-west Spain, it flowers from June onwards, sending up from its submerged stem a raceme of pretty, lipped, short-spurred pale yellow flowers to the sunlight. Beneath the water the finely segmented leaves carry the remarkable minute bladders which trap and digest small water creatures.

Associated with the insectivorous bladderworts, butterworts and sundews, by shallow mountain or lowland pool, lake edge or dune slack, are many typical aquatic plants, such as bog-bean *Menyanthes trifoliata*; pondweeds *Potamogeton* and *Polygonum* of several species; arrowhead *Sagittaria sagittifolia*, a very adaptable plant which can live virtually submerged in fast-running water, or on land which is almost dry after summer drought (it is rather local in Wales, but I have found its curious three-petalled white flowers in the latter habitat on Skokholm); and various floating, anchored or mud-loving crowfoots *Ranunculus* spp which will require working out with lens and handbook. Quillworts *Isoetes*, shoreweed *Littorella* and water lobelia *Lobelia dortmanna*, can be confused in the early stages of leafing, especially when lake water is high, but their flowers are quite distinctive as they emerge with the summer dwindling of water level. There are also innumerable, as it seems, sedges and rushes awaiting identification—not always easy even by the expert—in the freshwater habitats.

Where the water is deeper than about 6 ft the large white water-lily *Nymphaea alba* is absent; but it is apt to fill up shallower quiet waters which warm up considerably in summer, and is difficult to control. The smaller *N. a.* subspecies *minor*, which is common in lochs in northern Scotland, has occasionally been recorded in North Wales. The yellow water-lily *Nuphar lutea* is less common, but ascends higher to mountain lakes and pools.

It is remarkable how quickly an artificial pond fills with plant as well as animal life. If it is fed by a strong stream, seeds of water plants are soon flushed into it and take possession at whatever levels suit their ecological taste. An early arrival is the rootless but highly prolific duckweed *Lemna*, a plant which escapes the floods and frosts by producing turions (winter buds) which submerge and lie buried in the debris at the bottom until the water temperature rises in the spring. Frogbit *Hydrocharis* and water-soldier *Stratiotes aloides* are closely related freshwater plants which require lime in order to flourish, and have a curious life cycle. Frogbit is found floating chiefly in calcareous pools in South Wales, and produces turions instead of fruit. Only the female plant of water-soldier is normally found in Britain; its leaves gradually become encrusted with calcium carbonate and sink to the bottom in the autumn; in the spring new leaves, free of lime, shoot towards the surface. With no male to fertilise it the female plant produces runners, strawberry-wise, and these, breaking free, float off to establish independently.

Mistakenly I was once advised to introduce the Canadian pondweed *Elodea canadensis* into a large pond. It was supposed to help oxygenate the water and provide food and cover for fish. It certainly did—in three years it filled the 1 acre pond at all depths up to 4 ft! Pulling it up by the roots only causes the brittle stems to break into small sections, each of which can strike roots on touching bottom, for it too is female and multiplies entirely in this vegetative manner. It was first introduced into Britain about 1835. Fortunately it usually diminishes and even disappears, it is said, through loss of vigour or other biochemical factors which control its development; for instance it is said to have disappeared at present from Bala Lake.

The yellow flag *Iris pseudacorus*, reed *Phragmites communis*, and bulrush or reedmace *Typha* have each arrived on my ponds without my help, typical of common waterside plants which establish from seeds carried by wind, water or bird. The familiar velvety brown 'bottle' head of the reedmace contains the wind-pollinated flowers; the fruit remains intact on the neat brush all winter, splitting open raggedly early in the spring to spill its numerous seeds on wind and water.

Of the innumerable waterside grasses, sedges and rushes, there are two which are rare or scarce in Wales, but which I have had the luck to find: the flowering rush *Butomus umbellatus*, and the tall-growing sweet galingale *Cyperus longus*.

Fungi

The damp waysides and woodlands of Wales are well supplied with fungi; there is a wide field here for the amateur mycologist studying distribution and ecology, for the artist wishing to portray the more decorative, even for the epicure seeking the edible species. As scavengers of the vegetable kingdom fungi are both useful and destructive, whether they are large handsome-coloured parasites which invade plants and trees and reduce them to humus, or hidden species which break down the cellulose of timber man uses in buildings. Some (moulds) are essential to mature cheeses; some produce fungal diseases in man and his animals; but others, including penicillium, attack and break down harmful bacteria, virus and other parasites which cause diseases and which are often expelled in faeces (animal dung is a favourable habitat for a host of specialised fungal flora).

Late summer and autumn is the best period for a fungus foray. Of edible species in Wales the common mushroom *Agaricus campestris* and the horse mushroom *A. arvensis* abound; but the woodland agarics *A. silvicola* and *silvaticum* also taste excellent, and are common on pine-needles in coniferous woods. (Nor is man alone in cultivating edible fungi in dark cellars; the ant does the same.) The large parasol mushrooms flourish in Wales, the common *Lepiota procera* can be found even on windy cliff tops: the young caps (not the stalks) are delicious if peeled and cooked in butter or oil. Another rewarding gastronomic exercise is the preparation of the giant puffball *Calvatia gigantea* which, like all the puffballs, is good to eat while still young; the white flesh should be sliced and fried in egg and breadcrumbs. Strange to say the stinkhorn *Phallus impudicus*, close relative of the puffballs, is also edible in the young (egg) stage, although the smell of the mature fungus is off-putting; it is common in old woodlands.

Deciduous woods provide many handsome species, such as that artist's delight the orange peel fungus *Aleuria aurantia*, often 4 in across; it is edible. The conspicuous fly agaric *Amanita muscaria*, also a favourite subject for illustration, is, however, deadly poisonous, and so named because a fly-killing solution can be made from it. It is not a true agaric, but one of the many amanitaceae found in Welsh woodlands, of which the death cap *A. phalloides*, mistaken when young for an edible mushroom, has caused more fatalities than any other fungus. The false death cap *A. citrina* and the blusher *A. rubescens*, also very common, are nevertheless edible. There are many of the *Boletus* species in these damp woods, some poisonous, but the large cap mushroom *B. edulis* is eminently good to eat. Other interesting species are the chanterelle *Cantharellus cibarius*, the sundry edible waxcaps *Hygrophorus*, brittle caps *Psathyrella* with long fragile stems, and the vast fibrous projections of *Polyporus giganteus*, sometimes weighing many pounds, attached to the boles of hardwood trees.

Some of these are also found in coniferous woods, which do, however, have their own characteristic *Boletus*, *Tricholoma* and *Russula* species; also the saffron milkcap *Lactarius deliciosus*, the edible but sticky *Gomphidius glutinosus*, and the striking rose-pink *G. roseus*.

A few species are restricted to a single host tree or plant: such is the remarkable *Piptoporus betulinus*, found only on birch, a large smooth fungus which when dried has been used as a razorstrop, as blotting paper (sliced), and as tinder; it quickly destroys its host. The *Marasmius* species are a charmingly pretty group, and non-poisonous; they include the fairy ring champignon *M. oreades* growing on lawns and well-grazed grassland, which can be used as a culinary flavouring, since it keeps its piquant taste when hung up and dried like any herb; the woolly foot *M. peronatus*, found in beech woods—very peppery taste; *M. alliaceus*—garlic scented; and the most elegant little wheel toadstool *M. rotula*, growing on a long shining black stalk attached to decaying ground litter.

There are several good field guides to the identification of fungi: one of the best is by W. P. K. Findlay (1967) with excellent colour illustrations, including many by that dedicated mycologist, Beatrix Potter.

CHAPTER SIX

Other Wildlife

Amphibia and reptiles — Butterflies — Migratory
lepidoptera — Moths — Dragonflies — Bumble-bees
and others — Snails and slugs — Fishes

As MIGHT BE expected the small creeping and crawling forms of
animal life in Europe, such as the frogs, toads, newts, lizards and
snakes of the warmer south, were slow to advance into the
cooler north as the last ice caps melted from the land of Britain.
Some of these forms had not reached Wales, Scotland or Ireland
before England was separated from the Continent by the rising
level of the ocean, and Ireland became an island. In fact only two
species of the twelve which reached England are found indi-
genously in Ireland—the smooth newt and the common lizard,
although from time to time frogs and other species have been
introduced there by man.

There have also been releases in Britain of exotic southern
species, such as the edible frog *Rana esculenta*, the marsh frog
R. ridibunda, both now established in south-east England. The
wall lizard *Lacerta muralis* and the great green lizard *L. viridus*,
both common in the east of Jersey, have been introduced but
they have failed to survive anywhere for long in Britain. Pet
shops in Wales sell exotic species such as tree frog, midwife toad,
terrapin or pond tortoise, land tortoises, etc, but none has succeeded in establishing wild for even a third generation.

The species of amphibia and reptiles indigenous in Wales and
found in their appropriate habitats are nine, as follows:
Newts: warty newt *Triturus cristatus* and smooth newt *T. vul-*

garis: recorded chiefly from eastern and southern counties in Wales. More information on distribution and numbers is long overdue. The palmate species *T. helveticus* is the most abundant newt, quite numerous even in mountain country up to 2,000 ft, and on remote small islands, including Skokholm. In cool climates it is slow to mature and may breed in a relatively immature condition; this is known as neotony (in the high Alps the tadpole of this newt may be nearly a year in growing its four legs). Palmate newts can be found under stones hundreds of yards from their two main breeding ponds, but they will lay their eggs in quite small pools, which may dry out later in the summer. They can live long—up to a dozen years or more.

Common toad *Bufo bufo* Abundant in all counties. Numerous on Skomer, where at night in summer hundreds may be met crawling along the pathways, and a few descend to the shore to feed on sandhoppers along the tide-line. (The natterjack *B. calamita*, now found in south-west Ireland, is not indigenous in Wales, although it has been introduced occasionally, without much success.)

Common frog *Rana temporaria* Universally distributed, including Skokholm; absent from small pondless islands. Tends to disappear from ponds near towns, possibly because of pollution of water with detergents and pesticide residues; but still numerous in rural Wales. Often it will lay its eggs in the highest mountain peat pools, in an interval of mild weather between frost and snow, in early spring.

Common lizard *Lacerta vivipara* Common in all thirteen counties, occasionally up to 3,000 ft; also on Skomer, Ramsey, Bardsey, but not Skokholm. (The sand lizard *L. agilis* was formerly found in the sandhills of North Wales, but is now confined to Lancashire and Southern England.)

Slow-worm *Anguis fragilis* Common throughout Wales, from sea-level up to at least 1,000 ft. Particularly numerous in the west, in country lanes near the sea. Present on all but the smallest islands, that is on Skomer, Skokholm, Bardsey, Ramsey, Flatholm; but apparently not Grassholm or Middleholm. The name is apt: except when surprised on a warm day the slow-worm is slow moving, slow living, slow to mature (seven or eight years), slow to reproduce (one litter of up to eight young annually); becoming positively sluggish in cold weather. On Skokholm it liked to rest by day under wide boards or sheets of corrugated iron laid flat on the ground in warm dry situations. Here one very fine large dark-coloured female with a damaged tail lived for at least twelve years, and as she was mature when first recorded, she may have been approaching her twenty-first birthday. (A male in the Copenhagen Zoological Museum is recorded as mating at forty-five, and lived fifty-four years in captivity.) Grass snake *Natrix natrix*, also known as ringed snake; and viper or adder *Viperus berus*: both are common in suitable localities in all Welsh counties, although quite absent from any of the off-shore islets. Both hibernate at shade temperatures below about 8°C; but in warm spells even in winter they may come forth to bask, for both are sun lovers. In general the adder in Wales is commonest on the lower moors with heather, and south-facing slopes with rough open cover of gorse and broom, especially near the sea. Formerly it was abundant on Snowdon but is today much scarcer there, probably because of a series of cool wet summers, as well as the presence of numerous walkers and climbers whose first instinct is usually to kill any snake.

Grass snakes remain common chiefly in lowland valleys, where they hunt their principal food—frogs and other amphibians of the waterside; and they also swim after and devour minnows and other little fishes.

*   *   *

Wales lies at the centre of the whole British Isles, roughly midway between the warmer southern and eastern English summer and the cooler summer of Ireland and Scotland. In numbers of species, if not in numbers of individuals, insects are fewer in the cooler regions. In her strategic position Wales supports a medium number of insects, some of the northern, many of the southern, distribution. The entomologist can enjoy this situation of considerable variety, finding the southern continental types in the lowlands of South Wales, and the northern alpine species in the mountains of the north. There are a very few species which are almost, but not quite, confined to Wales today; and from time to time rare visitants turn up. But for the purposes of this book, it is more helpful to list only some of the more typical species.

Butterflies

Milkweed or monarch *Danaus plexippus* This migrant, which can cross the oceans in all directions from its North American home and has established itself recently in Australasia, has failed to colonise Europe. It is a rare occasional visitor, chiefly to South Wales.

Speckled wood *Pararge aegeria* A grass feeder, sometimes hibernating as a caterpillar. Common in woods and timbered country.

Wall brown *P. megera* Another grass feeder, found in similar country.

Marbled white *Melanargia galathea* This is a handsome southern species, not usually seen in Wales, but F. C. Best states that 'it inhabits all the South Wales counties up to and including Brecon, being most frequently found on the Carboniferous limestone'. There was a strong colony in Merioneth in 1964.

Grayling *Eumenis semele* Usually found in exposed dry sites, it is locally common. A unique dwarf race inhabits the Great Orme's Head, emerging somewhat earlier than the typical grayling which can be found only a short distance away on the sand dunes below.

Hedge brown *Maniola tithonus* This is a late summer butterfly, a real stay-at-home too, for it seldom strays more than a few hundred yards from where it was born. Widespread in Wales.

Meadow brown *M. jurtina* One of the commonest butterflies, emerging at midsummer and may be seen even on remote islets.

Small heath *Coenonympha pamphilus* Even more plentiful than the last.

Large heath *C. tullia* A northern species, breeding even in the Shetlands, it does not appear farther south in Wales than Tregaron Bog in the county of Cardigan, where it can be seen feeding at the white beak-sedge *Rhynchospora alba*; also at this plant in Borth Bog and other peaty places up to 2,000 ft.

Ringlet *Aphantopus hyperanthus* This very common butterfly varies in colour and eye-spots with each region. The female drops her eggs randomly in flight; the caterpillars seek various grasses to feed on, growing slowly all through the winter, without hibernation in the usual way.

Small pearl-bordered fritillary *Argynnis selene* and pearl-bordered fritillary *A. euphrosyne* are common in sheltered, wooded parts, where the caterpillars feed on sundry wild violets and pansies.

Dark green fritillary *A. aglaia* Fairly common, prefers more open country. Soon after hatching in August the caterpillars retreat to hibernate in the base of their food plant (*Viola*), emerging to feed in April.

High brown *A. adippe* and silver-washed *A. paphia* fritillaries are local but widely distributed in Welsh woodlands, both feeding on *Viola*.

Marsh fritillary *Euphydryas aurinia* This species requires devil's-bit scabious, a plant of marshy meadows and damp woods. On hatching from the cluster of eggs on the underleaf, the caterpillars spin a communal shelter-tent of silk under which they feed on the plant cuticle. Common where this plant is plentiful.

Red admiral *Vanessa atalanta* A migrant from the south, usually appearing in May; although many seek to overwinter in sheds and houses, they cannot stand frost. Breeding freely on stinging nettle, the new generation must fly south to a warmer land or perish.

Painted lady *V. cardui* Coming from North Africa, it is a later arrival than the red admiral. The eggs are laid on thistle. This migrant has appeared at Grassholm; in some years it is scarce, in others abundant.

Small tortoiseshell *Aglais urticae* Hibernates, appearing in the first warm spell in March. Very common.

Large tortoiseshell *Nymphalis polychloros*   Very rare, even in England, but has been recorded recently from North Wales.

Peacock *N. io*   This handsome butterfly often hibernates in dark corners of hollow trees, old buildings, dense evergreens, making a hissing noise with its wings when roused in the hand. It appears with the first warmth of spring. The eggs are laid on nettle, the caterpillars spinning a protective tent on hatching.

Camberwell beauty *N. antiopa*   Rare and irregular migrant from Europe.

Comma *Polygonia c-album*   Once confined, more or less, to the Wye Valley, this ragged-winged butterfly suddenly began to spread, during the present century, over Wales and the southern half of England.

Purple emperor *Apatura iris*   Rare, but found occasionally in Wales, chiefly in extensive forest areas of the Hereford and Monmouth borders.

White admiral *Limenitis camilla*   Slowly spreading north-west-wards, this forest species has reached the Forest of Dean and Monmouth.

Duke of Burgundy *Hamearis lucina*   This little speckled creature is very local, chiefly recorded in the south.

Small blue *Cupido minimus* and the silver-studded blue *Plebejus argus* are both principally coastal species in Wales, rather local, and variable in form.

Brown argus *Aricia agestis*   Most easily found on coastal lime-stone and sandhills.

Common blue *Polyommatus icarus*   Numerous, even on remote islands.

Holly blue *Celastrina argiolus*   Common but in more sophisti-cated habitat, including town parks and gardens.

Small copper *Lycaena phlaeas*   Common in open situations wher-ever sorrel *Rumex* species provide the caterpillar's food plant.

Green hairstreak *Callophrys rubi*   The greenish caterpillars of this common butterfly feed on gorse, broom, rock rose and bramble in lowland haunts, but chiefly on bilberry on the upland moors.

Brown hairstreak *Thecla betulae* Despite its specific name the
larvae does not feed on beech, but only blackthorn. It is extremely local anywhere, a southern continental species, but I
have found it in the Dovey Valley and Monmouthshire; and it
turns up locally in wooded areas elsewhere.

Purple hairstreak *T. quercus* Lives up to its specific name by
haunting oak woods. Like the other hairstreaks, the female lays
her eggs at the base of next year's buds; and on hatching in
spring the tiny larvae bore into the bud itself, and feed at first in
the shelter of the unopened ball of leaves. Common, sometimes
as much as to defoliate oaks.

White-lettered hairstreak *Strymonidia w-album* Closely resembles the last superficially, but feeds only on elm leaves,
especially wych elm. Rare and erratic in appearance, it has been
seen most frequently in Welsh border counties.

Large white *Pieris brassicae*, small white *P. rapae*, and green-
veined white *P. napi* are all too abundant to merit further notice
here.

Bath white *Pontia daplidice* In good years this migrant flies from
the Mediterranean to Britain, but so rarely reaches Wales that it
is a very special occasion, usually late in very fine summers.

Orange-tip *Anthocharis cardamines* Generally distributed. Occasionally the female may carry orange markings. Albinoes have
been collected.

The clouded yellows *Colias* are somewhat confusing. They are
migrants from the south, and visit Wales in fine summers,
making for clover, vetch, lucerne and others of the pea family.
In Wales *C. croceus* has often been recorded, and I have seen it
flying south in autumn over the sea near Skokholm.

Brimstone *Gonepteryx rhamni* Rather uncommon in Wales,
except where there is plenty of buckthorn *Rhamnus*, its food
plant. Hibernating late in the autumn the new generation
emerges early in the spring. Normally only the male is brimstone, the female is greenish-white; but one may see gynandro-
morphs in Wales, one side brimstone male, the other wing
greenish-white female.

Wood white *Leptidea sinapis*   Rare but has been recorded on leguminous plants from secluded woods in border counties.

Dingy skipper *Erynnis tages*, grizzled skipper *Pyrgus malvae*, and large skipper *Ochlodes venata*   All plentiful, but the small skipper *Thymelicus sylvestris* is scarce and chiefly seen in the southern half of Wales.

Migratory lepidoptera

During summer and autumn there is often a considerable passage of certain butterflies and moths migrating over Wales. This is particularly striking in calm sunlit weather when they may cross high above mountain tops and over small islands off the coast. Painted lady, peacock and red admiral butterflies are regular migrants, but the most spectacular is the large white. On some days the last appears in a mass movement, from sea-level to as high as the eye can recognise the dancing specks. If the wind is off the land, which is frequently the case in fine weather in Wales, thousands may be seen drifting out to sea in a westerly direction, towards Ireland and the open Atlantic—some heading apparently for the West Indies.

Of the moths the diurnal silver Y *Plusia gamma* is in some summers so abundant on migration as to swarm in thousands on rocks and islets at sea, temporarily resting. Usually it flies north in May and June; the new generation moves south from August to October, augmented by immigrants from northern Europe.

Of the eighteen British hawk moths nine are immigrants which cannot survive our winters; but only three of these are common in Wales. The hummingbird hawk *Macroglossum stellatarum* is a regular arrival, in some years quite common from June to September. The splendid convolvulus hawk *Herse convolvuli*, which makes a loud humming on the wing, appears at intervals, and I have captured it at Skokholm. The death's-head hawk *Acherontia atropos* is scarcer.

Moths

Other hawk moths are resident. But as there are over 2,000 species of moths on the British list, and the distribution of many of these is imperfectly known, there is plenty of scope for the moth-hunter in Wales. Nights with the mercury vapour lamp in border woodlands have proved so profitable that it has taken even the experts many days' work to identify all the catch. Recently some attention has been paid to the smaller catches taken by lamp at high elevations in Wales. H. N. Michaelis gives an account (*Nature in Wales*, September 1969), with notes on their food plants, showing that heather and bilberry support a surprising number, and a few even feed on cowberry—on the highest tops. It is always a surprise to find the large often hairy caterpillars of certain moths abroad in daylight, ambling and looping their way over the windy treeless moorland—for instance, true lovers knot *Lycophelia varia*, beautiful yellow underwing *Noctua pronuba*, double striped pug *Gymnoscelis pumilata*, small autumnal carpet *Oporinia filigrammaria*, and many others such as the emperor, fox, drinker, ruby and wood tigers, northern rustic, and the abundant antler moths. On willow and other *salix* bushes and trees, high up the mountain, eyed and poplar hawk moths are quite common.

Burnet *Zygaena* and forester *Procris* moths are conspicuous from their habit of flying in the sun and living in colonies. The burnets have crimson hindwings and black bodies. Some of these *Zygaena* are difficult to determine, and one subspecies—the transparent burnet *Z. purpuralis*—is only known from Abersoch, Carnarvon: its food plant is thyme—the Welsh race is *segontii*, distinct from local races in the Hebrides and West of Ireland.

The striking forester moths have metallic-green forewings and grey hindwings. The common forester *P. statices* caterpillar feeds on sorrel and is local in damp sheltered places on the edges of Welsh woods. The little cistus forester is confined to calcareous soils and in Wales is found only on rockrose growing on the Great Orme.

K

Another rare moth, unique to Britain and found only in North Wales, is the weaver's wave *Sterrha eburnata*. In 1965 great excitement was caused by the capture in North Wales of a single rosy marsh moth *Coenophila subrosea*, a species which vanished from the British Isles about 1851. Fortunately it has been reported again, in some abundance, from West Wales.

Dragonflies

For many years Bryan L. Sage has been compiling the recent records of dragonflies in Wales; these have been summarised periodically in *Nature in Wales*. The numerous small lakes, ponds and pools attract some two dozen common species, as well as some rarities. The splendid golden-ringed *Cordulegaster boltoni* is found at all levels from the sea (occasionally on offshore islands) to 2,000 ft. The emperor *Anax imperator* is confined to South Wales. The blue damsel-fly *Enallagma cyathigerum* and the common *Coenagrion* spp of damsel-fly are numerous.

The common *Ischnura elegans* even deposits its eggs in the little ponds on Skomer and Skokholm Islands, where migrant dragonflies appear from time to time. The rare, strongly migratory, yellow-winged *Sympetrum flaveolum* has reached Skokholm (29 August 1955), its most westerly record in the British Isles. Several other *Sympetrums* are regular migrants which breed in Wales.

Bumble-bees and others

The large *Bombus terrestris* and *B. lucorum* are common bumble-bees throughout Wales, and with them of course their dependents the parasitic *Psithyrus* bumble-bees, *P. vestalis* and *P. bohemicus*. First to emerge in the spring in Wales is the small queen of *B. pratorum*, leaving her hibernaculum in the sheltered south-west often quite early in March on a mild day; I have caught this and other common bumble-bees at sea between Skokholm and the mainland of Pembrokeshire. Its parasite is

P. sylvestris, which, like all 'cuckoo' bumble-bees herself unable
to collect pollen or produce her own workers to feed her offspring, lays her queen and drone eggs in the nest already established by the hard-working *B. pratorum* queen. Cuckoo bumble-
bees closely resemble the species they dupe, and in addition, if it
comes to a fight in the nest *Psithyrus* is heavily protected against
stings by tougher 'armour plate' than her host wears; in addition
to these hard plates of cuticle which cover her body, she has a
longer sting.

B. *lapidarius*, with its rufous tail, is abundant, along with its
remarkably similar rufous-tailed powerful cuckoo bee *P. rupestris*. B. *lapponicus* is an upland bee restricted to mountains in
Wales; but much more needs to be discovered about the distribution of the two dozen British bumble-bees and their parasites.
Thus the two similar species B. *humilis* and B. *muscorum* are both
found in Wales, but are frequently confused, as both have variable local forms. And there is the curious distribution of B.
smithianus, which has several colour forms and is found on small
islands round our coasts, from the Shetlands to the Channel
Islands, but not apparently in Wales; perhaps after all it is only
an insular form of B. *muscorum*, which it closely resembles.

Altogether in Britain there are some seventy species of social
insects, including other kinds of bees, the wasps and the ants,
within the great order Hymenoptera. But even more numerous
are the solitary bees and wasps within this huge order; and their
distribution—and that of most of the vast insect legion—in
Wales is most imperfectly known. I can only conclude this
chapter here with some notes on the more striking of the insects
which I have encountered in Wales.

The large wasp known as the hornet *Vespa crabro* was present
on my Monmouth farm forty years ago; it is still present in the
south-east of Wales, notably in the warm Wye Valley.

The great green grasshopper *Phasgonura viridissima* survives
thinly along the coast of South Wales, where it may be seen in
dunes and on sunny cliff slopes.

The glow-worm *Lampyris noctiluca*, disappearing from many

rural areas close to towns, is fairly common in country valleys, on bracken-clothed hillsides, and—curiously enough—it is abundant on treeless Skomer Island. The 'glow' of this beetle is produced by the wingless female, and one dark night in North Wales when I held one up to the small print of a page in a book the glow-worm produced enough light to illuminate a poem, line by line. The larva is carnivorous, feeding on snails and slugs.

The list of Welsh coleoptera is formidable. An interesting account of beetles found at or above 2,000 ft in Wales is given by R. Goodier in *Nature in Wales*, Vol 11, No 2 (1967). The same author writes of Welsh mountain spiders in that journal (Vol 10, No 3, 1968); and shows that there are at least thirteen Welsh spiders which elsewhere have a strictly arctic or alpine type of distribution.

Snails and slugs

About 180 species of non-marine molluscs are known living in the British Isles, of which thirty-five have not been found alive in Wales. Although further collecting should swell the list, most of the absentees are unlikely to be found. I am grateful to S. P. Dance for the following notes on these animals.

Molluscs flourish best in localities rich in lime (calcium carbonate being an essential ingredient of most molluscan shells) where food is abundant and the climate congenial. Consequently Wales is not a paradise for molluscs. The limestone ringing Glamorgan and that which occurs in Denbigh and a few other areas in Wales constitutes a mere fraction of the total land surface. A comparison of the molluscan and plant records for Glamorgan and Cardigan shows what a difference the presence of limestone makes to the fauna and flora. Those for Glamorgan are excelled by scarcely any other county in the British Isles, including the lime-saturated counties of south-east England; Cardigan's records are more akin to those for the unproductive counties of northern Scotland.

In addition there are extensive sand-dune formations which

provide a fairly lime-rich environment. On dunes near the sea at Merthyr Mawr, Kenfig and Porthcawl in Glamorgan, and Tenby, Manorbier and Stacpole in Pembrokeshire, the sandhill snail *Theba pisana* is locally abundant, sometimes producing large specimens up to 25 mm in diameter. The pointed snail *Cochlicella acuta*, the wrinkled snail *Helicella caperata*, the banded snail *H. itala*, are locally abundant on these dunes also. The grove snail *Cepaea nemoralis* is fairly widespread in Wales; this is a polymorphic species, with individuals of yellow or pink, and banded or unbanded, and brown phenotypes. At Newborough Warren nature reserve (page 193) *C. nemoralis* in these varied forms occurs sporadically in dense populations chiefly in areas of dune colonised by creeping willow; here Peter O'Donald (see *Nature in Wales*, 1968, Vol 11, pp 82–4) found that glow-worms were feeding, by a two to one preference, on the brown phenotype of this snail, a selectivity he could not explain.

The common snail *Helix aspersa* is locally abundant, particularly in the shelter of the stone-walled hedges of limestone and old red sandstone; it is the curse of those whose gardens are surrounded by such stone shelter. On the other hand the wall whorl snail *Vertigo pusilla* is a rare snail in Wales, restricted to stone walls in Merioneth and Caernarvon, but found recently in a dune slack and on a nearby ivy-covered wall at Merthyr Mawr. Shell pockets at Oxwich (page 185) have produced dead but fresh shells of the narrow-mouthed whorl snail *V. angustior*—a species not known living in Wales. On some steep, barren cliffs of St Bride's Bay the green hairy snail *Hygromia subvirescens* is abundant under cocksfoot grass and on hawkbit.

The rounded snail *Discus rotundatus*, arguably the commonest snail in the British Isles, occurs plentifully in woods, hedges and on rocks. The glass snail *Oxychilus draparnaldi* has long been known as a 'wild' species in Glamorgan, but elsewhere it lives close to human habitations. The round-mouthed snail *Pomatias elegans* is never found away from calcareous areas, where it is locally abundant. The lapidary snail *Helicigona lapicida* and the greater pellucid glass snail *Vitrina major* are rare and hard to find, but occur in southern counties. Rare too is the plaited snail *Acanthinula lamellata*, recorded from five counties, and common in at least one spot—on wet leaves at the Torrent Walk, Dolgellau. Close by, Charles Oldham discovered the mountain whorl snail *Vertigo alpestris* on an ivy-covered wall, where it still survives, and it lives elsewhere in this district; apart from Dolgellau it is known only from northern England and the Isle of Mull.

Slugs are found everywhere in Wales. The large black slug *Arion ater* is sometimes the only mollusc obvious, especially in the mountain region where the entirely black form variety *aterrima* Roebuck is prevalent. The ash-black slug *Limax cinereoniger* is not confined to old woodland and uncultivated lowland as is generally supposed; it lives on rocks in Pembroke, Radnor and elsewhere; in May 1969 one was found on rock in Cwm Cau high up on Cader Idris. The tender slug *L. tenellus* is, however, an old-woodland dweller, rather rare, but known in Monmouth, Brecon and Montgomery. Three shelled slugs of the genus *Testacella* have been recorded; and these, as well as other species, which are thought to be rare at present, are likely to prove more widespread than the records indicate—if only more persons were to collect and study them.

The freshwater species are interesting as they include some which have been able to colonise the cold high mountain ponds and llyns; and there are some rare lowland forms. River mussels *Unio* are hard to find, there being limited sources of hard water. The pearl mussel *Margaritifera margaritifera* is a soft-water species, well known as living in rivers and streams of the north where, as in the Conway River, it has been fished for its yield of pearl for centuries. Owing to pollution it seems to have disappeared altogether from Glamorgan rivers and streams. The oblong orb mussel *Sphaerium transversum*, an introduced North American species, has been found in the Shropshire Union Canal (page 179).

Charles Oldham found the tiny Arctic-alpine pea mussel *Pisidium conventus* in small llyns on the Snowdon massif; and Lilljeborg's pea mussel *P. lilljeborgii*, which lives in similar places, also occurs as far south as Glamorgan. The somewhat acid water of Bala Lake has a limited molluscan fauna, but it includes the rare glutinous snail *Myxas glutinosa* which is unknown elsewhere in Wales. By contrast Llangorse Lake with its high calcium content is rich in gastropods and bivalves: four species of *Lymnaea* occur, including huge numbers of the great pond snail *L. stagnalis*; the lake limpet *Acroloxus lacustris*, the great ram's-horn snail *Planorbarius corneus*, valve shells *Valvata*, the horny orb mussel *Sphaerium corneum*, pea mussels, the painter's mussel *Unio pictorum*, and the large swan mussel *Anodonta cygnea* are likewise common there. The duck mussel *A. anatina* inhabits Bosherston Pools in Pembrokeshire.

There are several bladder snails *Physa* living in Wales, especially in artificial habitats such as castle moats; but only one of them is indigenous, the others are almost certainly adventitious imports from North America. The trumpet ram's-horn snail *Menetus dilatatus*, also from North America, was found in May 1969 in Trawsfynydd Reservoir (page 196), the site of Britain's only nuclear power station which uses fresh water to cool its reactors; it lives here on rocks and submerged plants by the shore. Known previously from canals in the Manchester area, its occurrence at Trawsfynydd may be explained by the presence there of artificially warmed water in which this tiny snail seems to thrive.

Fishes

From their original home in the sea the present freshwater fishes have evolved into two categories: landbound or sedentary; and migratory to salt water. The larger Welsh rivers of the Severn, Wye, Usk, Towy, Teifi, Dovey, Clwyd and Conway and their tributaries, as well as some smaller rivers unpolluted by industrial wastes, are justly famous for their salmon, sea-trout and brown trout. The last two are varieties of the same species *Salmo trutta*. Known in Wales as the *sewin* or *sewen*, the sea-trout is the migratory form of the brown. All three *Salmo* species deposit their eggs in the gravelly bed of headwater streams.

The following freshwater fish are also found in Wales: bream, tench, carp, roach, dace, perch, river lamprey, miller's thumb, loach, pike, grayling, rudd, chub, minnow, gudgeon, bleak, ruffe, barbel. Most of these have been recorded from the Severn and its tributaries and the smaller rivers have some fewer species. Sticklebacks, which will also enter salt water, are common: the three-spined and the ten-spined breed freely in Welsh streams and large ponds.

Two fish are peculiar to Wales. In cold deep lakes in Snowdonia, such as Bodlyn, Cwellyn, Padarn, Llanberis, the char or *torgoch* (red-bellied one), really a land-locked species of salmon, is very close to the char which is found in the Lake District. More distinctive, and having no other than its Welsh name of *gwyniad* (gwyn = white), is a species of whitefish found only in Bala Lake; it is not a sporting fish, and normally can only be taken in nets. George Bolam gives a full description of this herring-like fish, which is 9–11 in long when adult, and is sometimes swallowed whole by the large pike (which he was told were first introduced into Bala Lake about 1803).

Eels, born in the Sargasso Sea, swarm into Welsh rivers and streams as wriggling elvers (they are then about three years old), and ascend to the highest pools and lakes, freely crossing land at night to reach waters which have little or no easy access from sea or river—as at Skokholm, where the ponds drain over sheer cliffs. Other sea fish which may swim far up river are: bass, flounder, grey mullet, smelt (chiefly in the Conway), lumpsucker. Burbot, allis and twaite shads, and sturgeon are rarer visitors, most frequent in the Severn. That voracious predator of edible and sporting fish, the sea lamprey, also ascends the lower reaches.

CHAPTER SEVEN

Places to visit

National parks – Nature reserves and other sites – Field Study Centres

APART FROM THE personal discovery of specially attractive, quiet places for nature rambles, there are many nature reserves, officially designated as such, which are open to the naturalist in Wales. Some of these require permits of entry, as detailed below. Several are within the three Welsh National Parks. In addition I have listed sites fairly well known to local naturalists, places which although not official reserves are in effect reservoirs of wild life. Larger areas of open country, wooded terrain, mountain and sea coast, which offer scope to the naturalist, are also mentioned.

(In the list below, after the national parks, the many lakes (llyn) and reservoirs are placed in alphabetical order within the section on nature reserves, under those headings.)

National Parks

SNOWDONIA, North Wales   Area approximately 850 square miles (Map—Figure 10). Covers a region roughly corresponding to that of the ancient realm of Gwynedd, ruled by the Welsh Princes of Wales up to the thirteenth century. Specially attractive to climbers, walkers, geologists, botanists. The main features are the steep glaciated mountains built around the harder rocks of volcanic origin; the deep valley or cwm and morainic lake or llyn associated with the last Ice Age; and the bare and stony sheep-grazed upland moor and peat bog. The Devil's Kitchen (see page 140) displays the crystalline lavas near its summit, and the rock faces here are famous for rare plants including the mountain spiderwort or Snowdon lily *Lloydia serotina*, unique Welsh flower of the hanging gardens of arctic-alpine flora in these highest mountains of England and Wales.

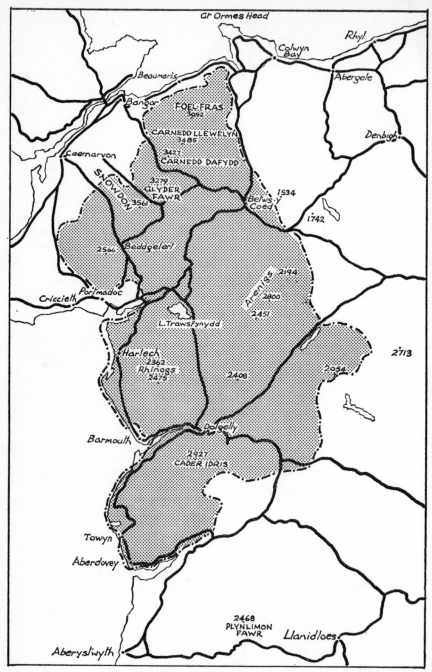

Figure 10 Map of the Snowdonia National Park

The Arenig mountains of Merioneth exhibit a structure typical of the rest of Snowdonia: alternate beds of volcanic ash and lava flow. These continue south to the splendid north-facing cliffs of Cader Idris.

The natural history is chiefly alpine, moorland, hill, peat bog and llyn or lake, the last often quite deep. The Park is the headquarters in Wales of the rare pine marten (page 46); and polecats also breed in the region.

There are at present thirteen declared nature reserves within the Park; each is described below.

PEMBROKESHIRE COAST NATIONAL PARK   Area approximately 225 square miles (Map—Figure 11). Ideal for the study of marine and maritime life generally, and archaeology. Geologically the north coast exhibits mainly ancient igneous rock types showing signs of glaciation; at St Davids, pre-Cambrian beds with earliest forms of giant fossil tribolites. The northern half of the Park carries its boundary inland to include the 1,760 ft Presely Mountain with its rhyolite and dolerite outcrops from which were transported, nearly 4,000 years ago, most of the stones forming the inner ring of Stonehenge on Salisbury Plain (page 32). The south coast is geologically newer, with Old Red Sandstone, and exposures of Carboniferous Limestone remarkable for cave formations (bones of prehistoric animals) and fossils of fish and marine shells.

The upper reaches of Milford Haven form a separate part of the Park, part of a drowned and drowning valley, of which the deepwater port of Milford Haven is the seaward portion. This upper area, around the Cleddau river system, forms a sheltered wooded refuge for many interesting birds and estuarine plants, and can be explored afoot or in a small boat.

The outer coast is rich in wildlife. Grey seals and sea-birds abound, and are best seen on visits to the island sanctuaries (see below) of Skomer, Skokholm, Ramsey, Grassholm, and St Margaret's, which are all nature reserves. There are several largely maritime plants of special interest, some rare, such as the prostrate broom, the perennial centaury and certain sea lavenders. The National Park coast footpath forms a splendid scenic walk and nature trail (descriptive leaflet from the address on page 221); it is well worth spending four or five days or more quietly exploring its total length, particularly wild and rewarding between Cardigan westwards to St Bride's Bay. The footpath along

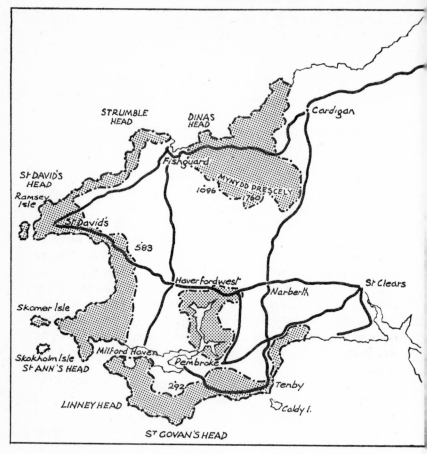

Figure 11   Map of the Pembrokeshire Coast National Park

the south coast is (temporarily we hope) interrupted between Bosherston and Freshwater West by a War Department firing range; this is a
limestone area very rich in wild flowers and sea-birds (see under Stack
Rocks), and striking rock formations of arch, blow-hole and cavern.

The whole coast of Pembrokeshire, as the OS maps show, is of
special interest to the archaeologist, with cliff forts (Iron Age type) on
almost every projecting headland, as well as cromlech, menhir and
standing stone of an earlier period; and inland are many prehistoric
burial mounds, Norman castles and medieval houses.

There are two Field Study Centres: Dale Fort, at the entrance to Milford Haven, ideal for the study of marine and maritime subjects; and Orielton, near Pembroke, an old manor house of Norman foundation in a woodland and small lake setting of 250 acres enclosed by high walls. The wildfowl decoy is near by, worked from the Orielton Centre.

As well as the island sanctuaries, several nature reserves are being set up, and some already managed, in Pembrokeshire. Details from the West Wales Naturalists' Trust (page 221).

BRECON BEACONS NATIONAL PARK   Area approximately 520 square miles (Map—Figure 12). Unspoilt, thinly populated, chiefly mountain area. Includes the heights of Carmarthen Van, 2,632 ft; Forest Fawr, 2,381 ft; Brecon Beacons, 2,906 ft, all in one chain; also, but separated by the vale of the upper Usk river, the eastern Black Mountains consisting of five main ridges, rising to a maximum height of 2,660 ft.

The geological strata is Palaeozoic, that is, the newer rocks of the Ordovician, Silurian, Devonian and Carboniferous systems. Predominating over the whole of the north-east of the Park, the Old Red Sandstone gives a pleasing warm, red colour to the ploughed earth and rock outcrops. Along the whole of the southern boundary the millstone grit touches the coal measures which provide the industrial wealth of the mining valleys south of the Park itself. Between the old red sandstone and the millstone the carboniferous limestone emerges to furnish the fine scenery around the rivers flowing south from the mountains. F. J. North's interesting book *The River Scenery at the Head of the Vale of Neath* describes in detail the tributaries of the river Nedd or Neath which, as they pass through the limestone, form a series of caves, swallow-holes, underground watercourses, and waterfalls unique in Britain. Members of the South Wales Caving Club and other cave exploration groups continue to explore these underground watercourses, and to find new chambers, halls and caverns deep in the limestone of this part of the Park. (A Park information leaflet is devoted to caving.)

The largest natural lake in the Park is Llangorse (Llyn Syfaddan) lying in the old red sandstone of the lower ground, a shallow rock basin scooped out by ice and dammed by a barrier of glacial gravel.

The natural history is largely described in the chapters on mammals,

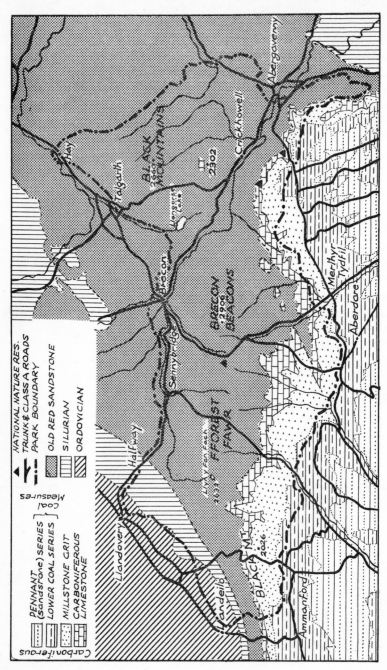

Figure 12   Map of the Brecon Beacons National Park

birds, flowers and insects. The very rare dragonfly *Ischnura pumilio* breeds in one place in the Park, and is known from only one other locality in Britain; and the bee-beetle *Trichius fasciatus* with its black-spotted buttercup-yellow elytra, an insect rare except in Wales and Scotland, may also be found here. The underground caverns of the limestone system support some blind semi-transparent crustaceans.

Much of the Park is covered by moorland, rather poor in variety of species. But there is a moderately rich limestone flora, particularly on the cliffs of Craig y Ciliau Nature Reserve. Here and at other limestone sites within the Park are the interesting whitebeams *Sorbus*, six species recorded, of which three are not known outside the Park (see page 141).

The nature reserves of Craig Cerrig Glesiad and Cwm Clydach are also within the Park.

Nature Reserves and other sites

Omitted from the annotated alphabetical list which follows are a number of small nature reserves, and sites of special scientific interest, most of which are in the care of local and regional conservation societies. Information about these is obtainable from the appropriate Naturalists' Trust (addresses on page 221).

Abbreviations:

FNR	Forest Nature Reserve
LR	Local reserve
NCNW	Refer to Nature Conservancy North Wales region
NCSW	Refer to Nature Conservancy South Wales Region
NNR	National Nature Reserve
OS	Ordnance Survey One-inch map sheet (number)
PA	Public access under the Countryside Act 1968
PRI	Privately owned site, restricted access
PVR	Permit to visit required
RSPB	Royal Society for the Protection of Birds

ALLT RHYD Y GROES Carmarthen and Cardigan OS 140 about 9 miles north of Llandovery, 153 acres. NNR PVR away from public path—NCSW. 81 acres of woodland, chiefly native sessile oak, on the steep banks of the Doethie river. The rest is moorland, scree and the rocky escarpment of Craig Ddu. Very beautiful country with tumbling streams.

Mammals: polecat, badger, fox, otter, red squirrel, etc
Birds: kite, buzzard, dipper, grey wagtail, ring ouzel, etc
Plants: ferns, mosses, liverworts, etc

ANGLESEY   Coast and lakes. See under: Cemlyn, Llyn Coron, Llywenan, Newborough Warren, Puffin Island, Skerries, South Stack.

BALA LAKE   See under *Lakes.*

BARDSEY   Caernarvon OS 115 2 miles off SW tip of Caerns, $1\frac{3}{4} \times \frac{1}{2}$ miles in extent, LR PVR and landing fee payable. Boats from Aberdaron.

Bardsey once had a community of a dozen small farms, a school, chapel and a so-called 'king'. Today it is grazed by one or two farmers renting the land from the owner, and is a nature reserve. Cristin farmhouse is the base for the Bird and Field Observatory established in 1953 by representatives of the West Wales Naturalists' Trust, the West Midland Bird Club and 'Friends of Bardsey' (particulars from the Hon. Secretary of the North Wales Naturalists' Trust). The Observatory welcomes visitors interested in all aspects of natural history, particularly birds, and bird migration, which are studied by ring-marking, with traps and mistnets. The Lighthouse attracts numerous migrants on misty nights.

Main features are the 500 ft eastern hill, with low cliffs at foot; the almost level western farmland; and the southern peninsula with the lighthouse and sandy harbour. The remains of St Mary's Abbey, built on the site of an early Celtic monastery, stand at the north end of the one road. There is a small stream connecting a series of withy beds originally planted to supply material for making lobster-pots, but which now form tiny plantations where migrants take cover and some species nest.

Mammals: grey seals and dolphins offshore.
Birds: raven, chough, razorbill, guillemot, shag, gulls, a few storm petrels and a large colony of Manx shearwaters. Spring and autumn migration can be exciting, often with large numbers of common species, and each year a number of rare birds, including some 'first records' for Wales, occasionally for the British Isles.
Plants: maritime, striking in spring, includes vernal squill.

BIRD ROCK (*Craig yr Aderyn*) Merioneth OS 127. A few miles inland from Towyn and the estuary of the Dysynni river, this bold rock catches the eye, more particularly in summer when it is the home of some two dozen pairs of nesting cormorants, their black forms standing like gargoyles, looking out over the flood plain of what was once a tidal marsh. LR which protects this otherwise unprotected bird; PVR but can be studied from the road with binoculars.

BLACKCLIFF & WYNDCLIFF Monmouth OS 155 2 miles north of Chepstow, 200 acres. FNR, access restricted to rides and trackways. Of special interest to botanists, this Forestry Commission property lies on carboniferous limestone, with rich varied herb layer under ash, beech, lime, yew and oak trees. Birds include three woodpeckers, pied flycatcher, redstart, buzzard, occasionally nightingale.

BORTH BOG (*Cors Fochno*) Cardigan OS 127. Borders south side of Dovey estuary (see page 184). Probably 2,000 acres of water meadows, quaking bog and partly reclaimed marsh, intersected with few roads and lanes. Much of it recently acquired to add to the Dovey NNR. NCSW.
Mammals: polecat, otter, fox, hare
Birds: various warblers, chats, buntings, buzzard breeding. In winter large numbers of duck and geese (up to 500 white-fronted—see page 96), snipe and wading species
Plants: three sundews, orchids and other marsh species

CADER IDRIS Merioneth OS 116 2 miles south of Dolgellau. Some 970 acres of this part of the Snowdonia Park is a NNR. PA except to the 50 acres of enclosed woodland, for which NCNW. Geologically of great interest for its Ordovician lava and ash flows, with fossil-bearing slate and mudstone. The approach can be made by the path above Dolgellau and the descent should be via the lovely Llyn Cau lying so spectacularly in the bowl of Cader; or vice versa.
Mammals: feral goat, polecat, badger, fox
Birds: buzzard, merlin, ring-ouzel and other mountain species
Plants: arctic-alpines on the heights; spignel or baldmoney *Meum athamanticum* here reaches the southern limit of its range in the UK

Canals (see notes on page 23). Welsh and English canals now come

L

under the government-sponsored British Waterways Board. Paid and voluntary workers have succeeded in cleaning and restoring to navigation many reaches of the few Welsh canals. Unfortunately there is now much motor-boat cruising on these rehabilitated waters, often resulting in pollution, muddying of water, dangerous wave-action on the banks, and deterioration of fish, bird and plant life, especially from June to September. In the spring there is less traffic, and this is the time to enjoy these navigable waters. But for the naturalist the still unreclaimed reaches are far more pleasing, since they form natural sanctuaries, with clear water rich in aquatic life.

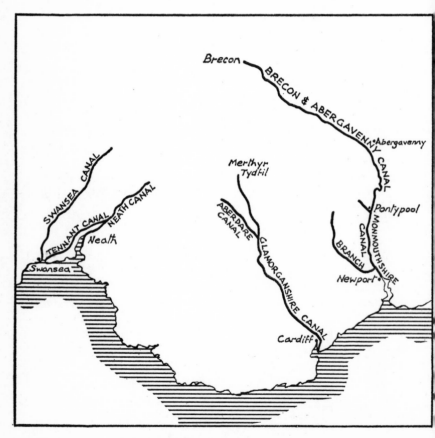

Figure 13   Canals in South Wales, now unused except for pleasure, some derelict

BRECON, ABERGAVENNY AND NEWPORT canal system (figure 13). Under restoration, much now available for boating. A very beautiful route through largely unspoilt country.

GLAMORGAN AND ABERDARE system (figure 13). Unreclaimed. Parts filled in but some reaches (eg above Whitchurch) delightfully overgrown and with clear water.

SHROPSHIRE UNION (formerly Ellesmere, Chester and Montgomeryshire canals) linking the Mersey with the Severn, and with the main English system (figure 14). The reach, Llangollen terminal to Welsh border, is now much in use by pleasure craft. The section south to Newtown is hardly touched so far, and most of this is wild and beautiful.

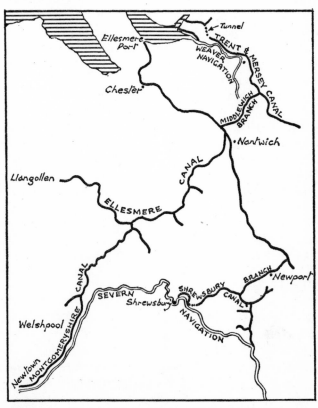

Figure 14   Canals in North Wales, and links with English canals

SWANSEA AND NEATH system (figure 13). Disused, dirty with industrial effluent, or filled in.

CARDIGAN ISLAND   Cardigan OS 139 about 4 miles NNW of Cardigan town, 40 acres. LR, PVR from West Wales Nats' Trust. A grassy islet grazed by a flock of Soay or Viking sheep controlled by the WWNT. Grey seals bask, and breed in caves near by. Breeding birds include cormorant, shag, oystercatcher, rock pipit, gulls.

CEMLYN   Anglesey OS 106 NW corner of Anglesey. LR PVR from North Wales Nats' Trust, or PA from public road and foreshore. The reserve area is about 60 acres and includes the large pool kept as a sanctuary by the late owner, which is brackish and separated from the sea by a shingle bar. The coast scenery westwards around Carmel Head is very fine and provides glimpses of the distant Skerries (see page 198). Birds: shelduck breeding; many species of duck and waders find refuge at other times. A strong migration of other species can be observed at this strategic coast station.
Plants: maritime species

CLWYDIAN HILLS   Flint/Denbigh OS 108. This range of low mountains has a comparatively dry climate (for Wales) and provides easy walking over rolling moors where upland species of birds can be watched, including grouse, buzzard, merlin, dipper, ring-ouzel, whinchat, pied flycatcher, grasshopper warbler, common sandpiper, raven.

COED CAMLYN   Merioneth OS 116 1 mile south of Ffestiniog, 157 acres. PVR from NCNW. This NNR is within the Snowdonia Park, and is typical of a sessile oakwood produced under the high rainfall of over 60 inches of the west coast. Herb layer of bilberry, molinia and mosses.

COED CYMERAU   Merioneth OS 116 1 mile NW of Ffestiniog, 65 acres. NNR within the Snowdonia Park. PA except away from public paths NCNW. This is a similar sessile oakwood, but in a ravine, with heavier rainfall—over 80 inches; a very beautiful mossy sanctuary best seen on a fine day. The Atlantic climate and high humidity favour an abundance of bryophytes of western oceanic species. The soil is acid overlying Cambrian sedimentary rocks.

COED DOLGARROG   Caernarvon OS 107 7 miles south of Conway, 170 acres. NNR within Snowdonia Park, with PA except away from paths—NCNW. This is another all-woodland reserve with largely oak cover, but as it is on the comparatively dry eastern slope of the Conway valley, the oaks tend to be intermediate in type between the sessile *Quercus petraea* and the common or pedunculate oak *Q. robur*. The varied rock types produce areas of beech and elm, and alder thrives in the damper ground.

COED GANLLWYD   Merioneth OS 116 5 miles north of Dolgellau, 59 acres. NNR within Snowdonia Park. As for Coed Cymerau, but includes the fine gorge of Rhaidr Du, with its famous waterfalls. Ferns, mosses and liverworts abound under the sessile oak canopy.

COED GORSWEN   Caernarvon OS 107 4 miles south of Conway, 33 acres of lowland oakwood very like that of Coed Dolgarrog, with fairly base-rich soil and good variety of ground plants.

COED RHEIDOL   Cardigan OS 127 10 miles ESE of Aberystwyth, 107 acres. NNR PA only on rights of way, NCSW. An all-woodland reserve within which 8 acres form a forest reserve (permit required to enter this) of sessile oak typical of the very humid conditions induced by high rainfall in a mild oceanic climate.
Mammals: polecat, fox, badger
Birds: buzzard, raven, pied flycatcher, redstart, wood warbler, etc
Plants: ferns, mosses, liverworts

COED TREMADOC   Caernarvon OS 116 1½ miles NE of Tremadoc, 49 acres. NNR PVR NCNW. All woodland covering steep screes and cliffs where ravens breed, and probably choughs. The base-rich rock types support a lime-tolerant flora. Part of the Snowdonia Park.

COEDYDD MAENTWROG   Merioneth OS 116 near Maentwrog, 169 acres. NNR within the Snowdonia Park, NCNW. Yet another oakwood, but with ground cover of bracken on north-facing slope.

COED Y RHYGEN   Merioneth OS 116 west side of Lake Trawsfynydd, 68 acres. NNR in the Snowdonia Park, PVR NCNW. About

750 ft above sea-level, the terrain is very rocky and ridged upon the almost soilless Cambrian grit, part of the Harlech Dome (as geologists have called this upland region of the Rhinogs). The reserve is an isolated woodland of stunted sessile oak, birch, rowan, hawthorn and ash, with some hazel; the heavy rainfall encourages a variety of ferns, many hanging from the trees.

Mammals: polecat, marten, fox
Birds: buzzard, pied flycatcher, redstart, warblers
Plants: include the filmy ferns and some rarer ferns

CORS GOCH   Anglesey OS 106, 103 acres of fen and heath, PVR NWNT.

CORS TREGARON (Tregaron Bog)   OS 127/140 12 miles SE of Aberystwyth. NNR also a Wildfowl Refuge, now extending to 1,898 acres covering the swampy flood plain of the Upper Teifi river, PVR NCSW. Often quoted as the best developed and finest example of a raised bog in England and Wales. Good views from the B4343 road north from Tregaron. Full time NC warden.

Mammals: polecat (common) including a reddish variety, otter, fox, badger, hare, etc
Birds: buzzard, kite, curlew, snipe, common sandpiper, redshank, teal and other ducks breeding. White-fronted geese and many duck visit and stay in winter, when peregrine and hen harriers are seen.
Plants: sundews, butterworts, and bog plant communities

CRAIG CERRIG GLESIAD   Brecon OS 141 6 miles SW of Brecon, 698 acres. NNR in the Brecon Beacons Park, PVR NCSW. Contains the two Old Red Sandstone crags of Craig Cerrig Glesiad and Craig Cwm Du, which are remarkable as the most southerly limit of arctic-alpine plants in Britain. The cliffs are surrounded by sheep-grazed moors.

Birds: peregrine, merlin, buzzard, raven, red grouse, ring-ouzel, common sandpiper, wheatear, dipper
Plants: arctic-alpines in the crags; moorland and peat bog species

CRAIG Y CILIAU   Brecon OS 141 2½ miles SW of Crickhowell, 157 acres. NNR in Brecon Beacons Park. PA except for the cave, for which NCSW. A limestone outcrop with endemic species of whitebeam growing on the cliff face (see page 141), also beech and lime. At the foot of the main escarpment near Llangattock is the entrance to the *Agen Alltwedd Cave*, the longest in the British Isles, 9 miles of passages with beautiful formations of selenite crystals, stalactite and stalagmite.

CWM CLYDACH Brecon OS 141 6 miles W of Abergavanny, 50 acres. NNR in the Brecon Beacons Park, this woodland is remarkable for a rich flora developed in mature beechwoods growing naturally over the gorge: one is on base-rich soils of limestone, the other on more acid soils from the millstone grit. Farther west in Wales beech grows only as a planted tree.

CWM GLAS CRAFNANT Caernarvon OS 147 1½ miles NE of Capel Curig, 38 acres. NNR in the Snowdonia Park; PVR NCNW. Interesting example of a rocky hillside on igneous soil (lime-rich volcanic ash) supporting arctic-alpines at a comparatively low altitude in crags above the little, fenced, woodland of 5 acres where ash, hazel and hawthorn thrive because of the lime. This corrie or low *crib* is very beautiful on a fine day after rain, when the clouds vanish and the waterfalls roar down from the jagged walls. The perennial wood vetch *Vicia sylvatica* is a handsome sight in summer, hanging from the lower ledges.

CWM IDWAL Caernarvon OS 107 5 miles W of Capel Curig, 984 acres of NNR on land leased from the National Trust in the Snowdonia Park. The first reserve to be declared as such in Wales, and sacred to the memory of the early geologists and botanists. Its spectacular cliffs rise, from Llyn Idwal at 1,223 ft above sea-level, to 3,200 ft under Glyder Fawr, and are composed largely of Ordovician volcanic rocks. Most celebrated is the Devil's Kitchen or Black Hole (*Pwll Du*), for geologists a wonderful example of downfolded rocks and known as the Idwal syncline; for the botanists a hanging garden of rare arctic-alpines; for the climbers a challenge to practise their skill (sometimes to the detriment of the flowers on the ledges). Here in Cwm Idwal in 1831 Charles Darwin and Adam Sedgwick explored before the glacial theory was generally accepted. Darwin afterwards wrote, 'We spent many hours in Cwm Idwal, examining all the rocks with extreme care, as Sedgwick was anxious to find fossils in them; but neither of us saw a trace of the wonderful glacial phenomena all around us; we did not notice the plainly scored rocks, the perched boulders, the lateral and terminal moraines. Yet these are so conspicuous that, as I declared many years afterwards, a house burnt down by fire did not tell its story more plainly than did this valley.' Much earlier, in the late seventeenth century, the young botanist Edward Lloyd or Lhuyd ranged Snowdonia as few have done since, and eventually the unique Snowdon lily or mountain spiderwort was named, in honour of its finder, *Lloydia serotina*.

On a fine day it is worth exploring the high ground of the reserve and examining two small llyns—Clyd and Y Cwn—and the several crags where wild goats roam. Bog-bean and water lobelia are characteristic of these acid rocky cool mountain pools.

Mammals: feral goat, fox, polecat, stoat

Birds: raven, common sandpiper, dipper, grey wagtail, wheatear, ring-ouzel

Plants: arctic-alpines include mountain spiderwort, mossy saxifrage, moss campion, rose-root, globe flower, parsley fern (see page 169)

DALE   See under *Field Study Centers*, page 202.

DINAS HEAD   Pembroke OS 138/151 3½ miles E of Fishguard. Rises dramatically to 460 ft from the sea within the Pembrokeshire National Park, and the footpath follows the cliff-top, giving good views of coast and the inland mountains. Seals breed in caves below, and gulls, fulmar, razorbill, shag, oystercatcher, raven and buzzard in the cliffs. Wild flowers are good, including mimulus in the marsh which forms the isthmus.

DOVEY ESTUARY   Cardigan & Merioneth OS 127 6–10 miles SW of Machynlleth. NNR covering about 3,525 acres of unspoilt foreshore and saltmarsh, and with a further 327 acres protected near the mouth of this very fine estuary of the Dyfi river. The eastern part forms a Wildfowl Refuge. There is a resident warden. Limited PA on foot, full particulars NCSW (see also under *Ynyshir*, page 201).

Noted for its bird life, during winter up to 3,000 ducks have been counted, including golden-eye. White-fronted geese regularly winter here, and on the adjacent Borth Bog. Wading birds are numerous. In summer there are several pairs of shelduck nesting. Spartina grass has invaded the foreshore (page 146), which has many interesting maritime plants.

EYWOOD POOL   Radnor OS 129 3 miles S of Presteigne, about 18 acres. LR managed by the Hereford and Radnor Nature Trust; 14 acres of water, the rest bush scrub. Great crested grebes among other water birds. Access by arrangement with the Trust.

FLATHOLM ISLAND   Glamorgan OS 165 3 miles off Lavernock, 52 acres. An island owned by Trinity House, formerly with an isolation hospital. Since it was largely abandoned as a residential island gulls have greatly increased and there are probably at least 1,000 pairs of lesser black-backed and 750 pairs of herring gulls. Shelduck and rock pipit also nest. Access by boat from Penarth. Maritime plants.

GOWER coast   Glamorgan OS 152/153. The south coast is principally limestone cliffs with some sandy and rocky bays, terminating in the island of Worms Head. On the north coast are the extensive sand-flats of the Burry Estuary, and the NNR of Whiteford Burrows, National Trust property (see under Whiteford). Splendid walking country, to visit the following places:
   OXWICH BAY, NNR of 542 acres (27 woodland), PVR away from shore, NCSW; 9 miles W of Swansea. Wide variety of habitats: dunes, salt marsh, reed marsh, fresh water. Westerly limit of breeding reed warblers. Winter haunt of waders and ducks.
   PORT EYNON to WORM'S HEAD   OS 152 12–16 miles W of Swansea. Limestone cliffs rich in flowers, and geological and archaeological interest. Port Eynon Point belongs to the National Trust, and the adjacent Overton Cliffs, a local nature reserve, to the Glamorgan Naturalists' Trust, who also own the 87 acres of Sedgers Bank, another local reserve consisting of low-lying rocks subject to tide and suitable for rock birds on passage (rock pipits and wheatears breed). Goat's Hole, half way to Worm's Head, is the famous cave of the Red Lady of Paviland (page 30), an Old Stone Age burial, where the bones of contemporary mammoth, woolly rhino, cave bear, hyena, bison, wild horse, reindeer, etc, have also been excavated.
   WORM'S HEAD is a NNR, 116 acres (including a short stretch of the mainland approach cliffs). Cross at half to low tide only. The

steep south-facing slopes are well known to botanists for their lime-stone 'rarities'. The steep cliffs of the outer Head accommodate nest-ing gulls (herring, great and lesser black-backs, kittiwake), guillemot, razorbill, fulmar, puffin (now rare), and rock-pipit. Good migration offshore.

The Glamorgan Naturalists' Trust also maintains the local reserves of:

BROAD POOL, Cilibion   OS 153, 4¼ acres for wading and water birds, bog and water plants, including the fringed waterlily *Nymphoides peltata*, and bog myrtle.

CWM IVY WOODS   OS 152 near the Whiteford NNR, 18 acres of native deciduous woods with typical birds and plants.

GELLIHIR WOODS   OS 153 70 acres of ash, oak, elm and birch in central Gower.

ILSTON QUARRY   OS 153 14 acres in central Gower, preserved for its geological interest where carboniferous limestone showing clay alternates with crinoidal lime and thin coal seam; attractive pond, stream and wood.

LLANRHIDIAN HILL   OS 153 overlooking Burry Estuary, 7½ acres of scrubby grassland on limestone, with a quarry; good for plants and butterflies; woodland close by.

GRASSHOLM   Pembrokeshire OS 151 10 miles off SW Pembs, 21 acres. RSPB sanctuary managed by the West Wales Naturalists' Trust (apply for access particulars). Boats from St Davids, Martin-shaven, Solva or Milford Haven; landings only possible in very fine weather. Over 15,000 pairs of gannets, also many kittiwakes, herring and great black-back (few lesser black-back) gulls, shags, razorbills, guillemots, rock-pipits, few puffins, one pair ravens. Good small bird migration in suitable weather and season.

GREAT ORME'S HEAD   Caernarvon OS 107. The 'Marine Drive' from Llandudno gives access by car or foot to the main feature of steep limestone cliffs famous for plants, butterflies and sea-birds (shag, kitti-wake and other gulls, fulmar, puffin, razorbill, guillemot, rock-pipit). Raven and peregrine falcon (rare). A good site for observing spring and autumn migration. The cliffs are slippery and dangerous, but the road is excellent, and there is a heathy plateau on top.

GWAUN VALLEY Pembroke OS 138 E of Fishguard, in the Pemb Nat Park. A wooded *cwm* (valley) with rapid stream set in a backcloth of the mountain pasture (*gwaun*). Deciduous oak (a small acreage of which is preserved as a local reserve by the West Wales Naturalists' Trust) where wood warbler and buzzard breed, with grey wagtail and dipper in the brook. Sundews and other marsh plants in boggy meadows.

GWENFFRWD Carmarthen OS 140 10 miles N of Llandovery, 1,200 acres. RSPB reserve PVR RSPB. Resident warden. Woodland and moorland.
Mammals: fox, badger, polecat, red squirrel
Birds: kite, buzzard, merlin, pied flycatcher, redstart, wood warbler, dipper, ring-ouzel, common sandpiper, grey wagtail, etc
Plants: upland species, ferns, mosses, liverworts

KENFIG POOL Glamorgan OS 153 about 7 miles W of Bridgend, 70 acres. Efforts to establish a NR here have so far failed, and there is some disturbance with sailing at week-ends. As a result the Pool is best for wildfowl in winter, when large numbers of duck, and some bewick's and whooper swans visit. Botanically the surrounding dunes are noted for orchids: marsh, fen, and hybrids; helleborines, bee orchid, twayblade, wintergreen. Also one of the few stations in Britain for the mudwort *Limosella subulata*. Insect life interesting with butterflies, moths (including the variable *Aderis hastiana*), sand-wasps, sawflies and beetles of the sandy habitat.

Lakes (Llyn = Lake)

BALA Merioneth OS 117. Bala town is at the east end of this fine lake which is about 4 miles long, ½ mile wide. Within the Snowdonia Park, on the geologically and scenically famous Bala Fault stretching from Bala south-westwards to Talyllyn pass and lake and so to Towyn on the coast. The largest natural lake in Wales. George Bolam (1913) wrote much about Bala in his *Wild Life in Wales*, especially about its fish, which include large pike, perch and brown trout; but above all 'From time immemorial Bala Lake has enjoyed the distinction of numbering among its inhabitants the Powan, or Gwyniad (*Coregonus culpeoides*)' found nowhere else (see page 168);

this is a species of white fish the size of a small herring, and only taken in nets, spawning in spring, never entering rivers but spending much time in the deeper part of this comparatively deep lake.

Mammals: marten, polecat, otter, fox, badger, hare, water shrew, etc

Birds: buzzard, merlin, raven, grouse, grebes, sandpiper, kingfisher, and woodland and moorland species

Plants: the new lower shore-line provides some interesting colonists such as small meadow-rue *Thalictrum minus*, which likes damp shady sites and whose subspecies (probably *umbrosum* at Bala) are the despair of botanists who cannot decide if the numerous variations are genetical or arising from environmental influences, since the habitat of this yellow-flowering species varies from dry limestone rocks to open dunes and mountain lakes. It is also found on mountain cliffs with *T. alpinum*, the purple-flowering alpine meadow rue, which is a dwarf compared with *T. minus*. Shoreweed, awlwort, quillworts, water lobelia, and some interesting and rare sedges. The lowering of the lake level in recent years has seriously affected the ancient shore-line flora, alas.

CONWAY Caernarvon OS 107 7 miles S of Betws-y-Coed. Within the Snowdonia Park, and famous for its trout, once the preserve of the Lords of Penrhyn, and now a National Trust property. Some 25,820 acres of beautiful hills and valleys chiefly west of Ysbyty Ifan village (where there was a hospice of the Knights of St John) are included in this property, the haunt of mountain and lake species, and here you may glimpse the rare pine marten.

LLANGORSE Brecon OS 141 6 miles E of Brecon. Within the Brecon Beacons Park. Lies in a shallow rock basin scooped out by ice and dammed by a barrier of glacial gravel. Fed by the river Llynfi (draining northwards to the Wye) this large lake is rich in nutrients, and supports extensive reedbeds, plant and animal life. Sailing enthusiasts in summer have not improved the amenities for birds and there are fewer great crested grebes and ducks nesting. Reed warblers are numerous, and yellow and grey wagtails nest in wet meadows and by streams respectively. Overhead are buzzards and ravens and in the nearby river banks kingfisher and sand martin are characteristic breeders. Winter visitors include goosander, pintail, Canada goose, wild swans and migrant waders.

Plants: alder and willow and reeds shelter a rich flora of crowfoots and great spearwort, pondweeds, three species of duckweed, the

fringed waterlily, various species of polygonum, and the true white
and yellow waterlilies. (For molluscs, see page 164)

LLYN CORON Anglesey OS 106 near Bodorgan. PRI. A winter
resort of large numbers of wildfowl.

LLYN COWLYD Caernarvon OS 107 2½ miles N of Capel Curig.
One of the larger, and the deepest, Snowdonia Park lakes, long,
narrow, 222 ft deep; supplies Colwyn Bay with water and linked
with tunnel to Llyn Egiau over the mountain to the north. Egiau is
quite shallow, however. On a quiet sunny day a ramble from one
llyn to another is rewarding in scenery of crag and moorland, although birds are few, and water plants limited: quillworts, water
lobelia, flotegrass, starworts, floating bur-reed and pondweeds are
characteristic, with waterlilies flowering about midsummer.

LLYN IDWAL Caernarvon OS 107 5 miles W of Capel Curig
NNR, see Cwm Idwal.

LLYN LLYWENAN Anglesey OS 106 4 miles NE of valley. A
lane gives access to the lake, where tufted duck, shoveler, teal and
mallard breed in the reed beds. Many wildfowl including swans and
Canada geese visit in winter. There is a black-headed gull colony.

LLYN OGWEN, Nant Ffrancon Pass

LLYN PADARN, Pass of Llanberis

LLYN PERIS, Pass of Llanberis

All three accessible from the road alongside, in these narrow Snow-
donian valleys, with naked rocky crags and sloping sheep-grazed
edges. Chiefly of interest to trout fishermen; but Padarn and Peris
have the rather handsome local salmonid fish char, which likes fairly
deep water and spawns late in the autumn.

LLYN Y FAN FACH Carmarthen OS 140 about 10 miles SW of
Sennybridge. Accessible by lane and footpath from the picturesque
mountain village of Llanddeusant, following the Afon Sawdde
stream which drains this beautiful lake. This is almost encircled by
the towering 500 ft high red sandstone cliffs of the Carmarthen Van
or Black Mountain. There is a well-known legend which recounts
how a farmer falls in love with a fairy maiden who rows a golden
boat with silver oars upon the blue waters. He is allowed to marry
her on condition he promises not to strike her thrice with iron
(evidently an echo of the clash of the Bronze Age inhabitants with
the invading Iron Age tribes). She bears him three fine sons, but
growing careless with prosperity—for her fairy cattle have brought

him much wealth—he at last strikes her for the third time with an iron implement, whereupon she vanishes beneath the llyn, taking her cattle with her. However, mourning her sons, she reappears at intervals sufficiently to instruct them in her magic art of healing. Hence, it is said, the tradition of a race of local physicians famous for their secret knowledge of medicinal herbs. Successful cures of human ills with those herbs may well have included the use of arctic-alpines growing on the cliffs and screes above the llyn: purple saxifrage, least willow, campion sea, spring sandwort, globe flower, roseroot, cowberry, parsley and bladder and other ferns, mossy saxifrage; and the flora of the cool llyn—water lobelia, bog asphodel, quillwort, etc.

LLYN Y FAN FAWR lies due east of the last, a 2 mile walk under the screes of Banau Sir Gaer (Carmarthen Beacons), a slightly larger sheet of water nearly 2,000 ft above SL and, like the smaller llyn, a glacial lake held in place by a moraine; it is the source of the Tawe, which rushes southwards through desolate moorland, and can best be reached from the Swansea–Sennybridge road A4067, turning off at Glyntawe.

Birds: buzzard, merlin, peregrine, raven, red grouse, dipper, grey wagtail, sandpiper

TALLEY   Carmarthen OS 140 7 miles N of Llandilo along B3402. Two attractive lakes rich in aquatic life with abundant natural cover of reeds, waterlilies and shore vegetation, lying north of the remains of the twelfth-century Abbey founded by the Welsh prince Rhys ap Gruffydd. The wooded surroundings in this lowland vale are little explored.

Mammals: polecat (rare), otter, fox, badger, stoat

Birds: buzzard, great crested and little grebes, mallard, teal, kingfisher, pied flycatcher, redstart, reed bunting, grasshopper warbler, sedge warbler, etc

Plants: white and yellow waterlilies, water *ranunculus* spp, waterwort (*Elatine hexandra*), marsh speedwell, marsh red-rattle, gipsywort, and many others (see R. F. May, 1967)

TALYLLYN   Merioneth OS 127 8 miles S from Dolgellau. Geologically on the Bala fault line Bala–Towyn. A much-fished lake, shallow and good for brown trout. Few breeding birds, but good aquatic plants, including an intermediate yellow waterlily, a rare plant considered by some to be a cross between the common *Nuphar lutea* and the smaller *N. pumila*. On the north side of the lake Cader

Idris rises steeply, and the road to Dolgellau passes through a dramatic pass, sombre and stony, haunted by buzzards, ravens and
mountain birds, and wild goats on the crags.

LAVERNOCK POINT   Glamorgan OS 154 1 mile S of Penarth.
This headland is a good site for studying bird (and butterfly) migration
in the Bristol Channel, and some rare species have been recorded, such
as ortolan, red-breasted flycatcher, icterine and Bonelli's warblers. At
sea—skua, shearwater and petrel.

LLANDDWYN ISLAND   See under *Newborough Warren*

LLANGORSE   See under *Lakes*

LLYN   See *Lakes*

MAWDDACH ESTUARY (and river)   OS 116 S of Barmouth. At
low tide a stretch of richly golden sand, the inland part within the
Snowdonia Park, the river Mawddach rising far inland close to the
source of the east-flowing Dee. The whole river and estuary are rich in
wild life, and should be explored over several days. On the south side
of the estuary is *Arthog* bog, highly interesting botanically, where the
very beautiful wavy St John's wort *Hypericum undulatum* reaches its
northern limit in Europe (elsewhere only known from South Wales,
Cornwall and the Iberian peninsula and Azores). Orchids and crowfoots abound on this bog. Down by the shore there are salt marshes
with spartina threatening the native mixture of *festuca-puccinellia-
armeria* sward palatable to sheep, and here aster, sea lavender and sea
arrow-grass thrive along with the sea rush *Juncus maritimus*. In winter
the ducks, geese and wild swans find sanctuary; and shelduck, curlew,
snipe and lapwing breed near the shore.
    The high tide reaches to the river junction near Llanelltyd bridge and
one should follow the main road north to where the Mawddach turns
north-east towards the high moors of Dduallt (2,155 ft) through the
most beautiful wooded cwm, with waterfalls and hanging woods. Here
there are only bridleways, forest tracks and paths; if pursued eastwards
the route emerges into the cwm where the Lliw river flows into Bala
Lake.
Mammals: otter, fox, badger, polecat, dormouse, etc

Birds: buzzard, raven, pied flycatcher, wood warbler, redstart, wood-cock, snipe, curlew, teal, redshank, etc

Plants: varied, chiefly suited to acid conditions, the high land dominated by hardy grasses (mat, deer and cotton grasses) and rushes, with sun-dews, butterwort, bog asphodel and sedges; woodland largely sessile oak with ground flora including wild garlic, sanicle and tall brome grass

MILFORD HAVEN   Pembroke OS 151. (See under Pembrokeshire Coast National Park above.) The various tidal creeks (known locally as pills) of Dale, Angle, Pembroke, Cosheston, Carew, Cresswell, Garron, and the Cleddau river system provide a wintering ground in the mild climate for great numbers of duck and wading birds; and the flora is rich in maritime plants due to the varied rock types (chiefly limestone and old red sandstone) and topography of rock, sand, mud and salting along the foreshore.

Mammals: grey seal, otter

Birds: buzzard, raven, chough (outer coast), fulmar, gulls, shelduck, breed. Huge variety of duck, wader and other migratory species autumn to spring. Woodland species in the upper reaches, especially the Forestry Commission forests of Benton and Canaston

Plants: interesting sea lavenders, scurvy grasses, prostrate broom, and others described in chapter on Wild Flowers

MORFA DYFFRYN   Merioneth OS 116 3 miles SW of Harlech. A large area of mobile and fixed dunes of which 500 acres are a NNR, the whole within the Snowdonia Park. PVR away from public paths—NCNW. Chiefly remarkable for flora of mixed habitat—acid, cal-careous, saline and fresh water. Much studied by botanists, including Peter Benoit and Mary Richards, who describe the area and its plants in their book on the flora of Merioneth, 1963. The wet slacks between the dunes are rich in orchids, creeping willow, sedges and mosses. The dry fixed dunes have many attractive flowers such as field gentian, lady's fingers, autumn lady's tresses, burnet rose, blue fleabane, thyme, sea holly, sea campion, violas (including *V. canina* x *riviniana*, a very fine hybrid living happily with its parents) and maiden pink. Rarer plants are mentioned in the Benoit-Richards book.

Birds: nesting shelduck, redshank, oystercatcher, ringed plover, lapwing, snipe, reed bunting, skylark, meadow pipit, black-headed gull and little tern

Insects: dragonflies, butterflies, cinnabar and burnet moths abound; grasshoppers, beetles, snails (see page 164)

MORFA HARLECH Merioneth OS 116 N of Harlech. Similar to the last, a very large area of marram grass dunes, with slacks, of which 1,214 acres are a NNR, within the Snowdonia Park. PVR NCNW. Based on shingle banks extending north from what was once the seaport of Harlech, now a town with no sea outlet. Blown sand continues to build up the system of dunes under the prevailing westerly winds. Fauna and flora as for Morfa Dyffryn. (See also Traeth Bach.)

NEWBOROUGH WARREN Anglesey OS 106 S point of Anglesey. A NNR of 1,566 acres, including the rocky western point of Llanddwyn Island. As for the last two reserves, this is a large area of blown sand, biologically rich in species of plants and animals. There are four main ridges with mobile dunes extending about 1½ miles inland, much of it planted with conifers by the Forestry Commission. PA over rides and paths, PVR NCNW away from these. The reserve covers two estuaries with a large and growing salt marsh. Ynys Llanddwyn is accessible except at high tides, and is partly rocky, with a colony of shags on an islet offshore. The changes due to afforestation have been closely studied by the NC and other naturalists, and show a slow impoverishment of the flora as shade closes in; but bird species have increased in number as the average height of the plantation has risen. Thus breeding oystercatcher, stonechat, meadow pipit, skylark, curlew and lapwing, deprived of open dune land with scattered bushes, have disappeared with the trees reaching 15–18 ft, giving way then to nesting linnet, yellowhammer, reed bunting, wren, goldcrest, chaffinch, robin, wood pigeon, willow warbler, chiffchaff, redpoll, blue and great tits. After 18 ft the cover became too dense for linnet and yellowhammer, and there is further loss of bird species as this all-conifer forest matures, and reduces the ground flora to a few shade-resistant plants, mosses and fungi. The northern boundary of the reserve is the very fine estuary of Malltraeth Sands, with a freshwater pool convenient to study from the A4080 road; the whole much frequented by wildfowl and wading birds almost throughout the year.

Plants: apart from the changing sequence of the ground flora of the

M

growing conifer forest, the shore line (and the unplanted dunes) provide a good variety of maritime species, as rich if not richer than the Morfa dunes (above).

ORIELTON   Pembroke OS 151 3 miles SW of Pembroke, LR PVR. Part of the old walled estate is a farm, the rest, about 100 acres, is a nature reserve attached to the old manor house, now a Field Centre of the Field Studies Council (see page 201) where visiting naturalists are welcome to stay, and excellent facilities of laboratory and library available. The reserve area is chiefly regenerated woodland of oak, ash and elm, with some planted conifer, lake of 3 acres with water lilies, and outside the walls, the Duck Decoy lake, where wildfowl are ring-marked by cage-trapping. Orielton is in the centre of the Castlemartin peninsula, rich in archaeological sites and near the limestone cliffs (see *Stack Rocks*), and the flats of Angle Bay (wildfowl, waders, marine biology). Mammals: fox, badger, horse-shoe and other bats. Grey seals on coast
Birds: buzzard, raven, woodlark, nuthatch, kingfisher, etc
Plants: great variety within the peninsula, particularly 'Lusitanian' species, including rock sea lavenders; by lake, galingale, *Arum italicum*, Solomon's seal, monkshood.

OXWICH   See under *Gower*

PENMOELALLT   Brecon OS 141 3 miles N of Merthyr Tydfil, 17 acres. FNR of Forestry Commission. PA statutory trackways and rides. An interesting example of woodland and crag on carboniferous limestone close to coal measures. The crag and scree limestone is dominated by ash, elm and rowan with a few endemic *Sorbus* trees: *S. leyana* is present, very rare and only found elsewhere in Britain in the Brecon Beacons Park.

PRESELY MOUNTAINS   Pembroke OS 139 within the Pembs National Park. Smooth grassy moorland rising to 1,760 ft, with few rock outcrops. Of considerable archaeological interest (page 32) with stone circles, tumuli and fortified British hill (Foel Trigarn, 1,200 ft). Upland flowers, buzzard, raven, wheatear, curlew.

PUFFIN ISLAND   Anglesey OS 107. Most easterly point of Anglesey. Also known as Priestholm and in Welsh *Ynys Seiriol* (from the priest who built a cell there about 540). PRI, enquire at Beaumaris for boat, which is a good way to examine the island (without landing), overgrown in summer with tall herbage (see Lacey, *Nature in Wales*, 1957, pp 464–70, for description of flora). Few puffins are now left, but other sea-birds are good, especially gulls, shag, cormorant.

RAMSEY ISLAND Pembroke OS 151 near St Davids, 650 acres. RSPB reserve (National Trust covenant agreement), PVR RSPB. Landing fee 5s, boat from Porth Stinan (Lifeboat station). The spectacular high cliffs and caves at the back of the island are best seen from a boat (regular trips daily) in fine weather, giving close views of nesting auks and the large herd of grey seals. There is simple do-it-yourself accommodation at a hostel on the island for those who would study plants, bird migration (which is interesting and sometimes spectacular in spring and autumn), geology or marine biology.

Mammals: about 200 grey seal pups are born on caves and beaches, September to November inclusive; at other times there are assemblies and groups basking or fishing around the island

Birds: chough, raven, buzzard, peregrine falcon, razorbill, guillemot, kittiwake and other cliff-nesting gulls, oystercatcher, wheatear

Plants: little explored but somewhat conditioned by overgrazing by rabbits and rats except on off-islets (Stony Ynys Bery, without rodents, has a salt-resistant flora including showy masses of *Vicia cracca*).

Reservoirs

EGLWYS NUNNYD Glamorgan OS 153 near Margam, 260 acres. PVR apply Glamorgan Nats Trust. The largest sheet of fresh water in the county attracts many ducks, coots, grebes as non-breeding visitors, with passage of waders, gulls and terns.

LLANDEGFEDD Monmouth OS 155 3 miles S of Pontypool, 400 acres. PVR apply Monmouth Nats Trust. As for last reservoir—visiting birds.

LLYN BRIANNE Carmarthen 10 miles N of Llandovery, 4 miles long. A new reservoir, nearing completion with the publication of this book, and right in the heart of kite country. The dam site is (on OS 140) map reference SN 792484, and a new road links up the east side of the Towy with the lonely moorland road between Abergwesyn and Tregaron. Fauna and flora as for the adjacent reserves of Gwenffrwd and Allt Rhyd y Groes.

RHAIDR (Rhayader)   Brecon and Radnor OS 128 4 miles W of Rhayader. Birmingham Corporation constructed these long winding waterworks which drain into the Elan Valley. A good road winds around one side of the first three to reach the dam at the last and largest reservoir. In the woods and open moorland around there is much of interest.

Mammals: polecat, fox, badger, hare

Birds: kite, buzzard, merlin, grouse, ring-ouzel, dipper, sandpiper, curlew, snipe

Plants: upland and heath species

TAF FAWR and FECHAN VALLEY   Brecon OS 141 about 5 miles N of Merthyr. There are two reservoirs in each valley, draining south from the Brecon Beacons to serve Cardiff and other water boards. They are partly planted around with conifers, and stocked with brown and rainbow trout. Owing to their fluctuating level, often low in summer, they are not faunistically or floristically interesting, and too high and too far from the coast to attract many migrants. But dippers and grey wagtails nest by the Taf and its feeder streams, all sparkling and clear in contrast with the river's polluted state in the colliery area of Glamorgan below.

TAL-Y-BONT   OS 141 7 miles SE of Brecon, 300 acres. One of the more attractive reservoirs, with a good record of wildfowl present in winter, as well as grebes and waders, some of which may remain to breed (great crested and little grebe, common sandpiper, redshank suspected). Buzzard, raven, redstart, pied flycatcher, yellow wagtail nest nearby. Cormorants fish regularly, although they do not nest in the county. Wild swans and oystercatcher recorded annually.

TRAWSFYNYDD   Merioneth OS 116 11 miles N of Dolgellau. An artificially enlarged lake; water used for atomic power station cooling, causing local rise in the temperature near same. Good trout and perch fishing. The moorland country around is most attractive, within the Snowdonia Park, and includes Coed y Rhygen NNR on the western shore 7–800 ft above sea level (see page 181).

Mammals: polecat, perhaps marten, otter

Birds: black-headed gull, grebes, sandpiper, grey wagtail, dipper, ring-ouzel. Oystercatcher has nested. Many ducks and waders on migration. Tufted duck, pochard, and teal breed

Plants: many typical water plants, sundews, orchids, mosses, ferns, etc

VYRNWY LAKE   Montgomery OS 117 10 miles SW of Bala. Liverpool water supply has drowned a steep remote Welsh valley, the sides now clothed in planted forest. A splendid walk over the mountain road between Lakes Vyrnwy and Bala, with a variety of habitats.
Mammals: polecat, marten, otter, badger, fox, hare
Birds: buzzard, kite (rare), merlin, raven, dipper, ring-ouzel, siskin

RHINOGS   Merioneth OS 116 5 miles E of Harlech, 991 acres form a NNR. PA covering the peaks of Rhinog Fawr 2,362 ft, and Rhinog Fach 2,330 ft. The whole Rhinog range is fascinating country, much of it little-grazed and therefore deep in heather and bilberry, some of it hard going with boulders and large stones between which are hidden ankle-breaking fissures. There are numberless small pools and some sizeable llyns—the largest are fished for trout. The hard Cambrian rocks are acid and unproductive of many plant species, but lower down the streams and bogs are interesting with a richer flora with many ferns, and with dragonflies and butterflies. The archaeologist is delighted with the number of dolmens, stone circles, standing stones and burial mounds indicating a busy occupation 3–4,000 years ago, evidently in much better weather than the present rainy centuries!
Mammals: polecat, fox, badger, hare, a few feral goats
Birds: buzzard, raven, ring-ouzel, wheatear, sandpiper, teal, dunlin, merlin (rare), golden plover, etc
Plants: of acid rocks and bog, including lesser twayblade and mossy saxifrage

RHYD-Y-CRENAU   See under Field Centres, page 202.

ST DAVID'S HEAD   Pembroke OS 138 2½ miles NW of St David's. Within the Pembroke Park. Spectacular view point, and for the study of migrating sea birds. Grey seals pup in nearby caves and lie out on rocks. Along this wind-torn headland are many remains of stone huts and enclosures, and a burial chamber (cromlech) of the Neolithic period.
Birds: raven, chough, peregrine, buzzard, wheatear, rock dove, gulls
Plants: fine display of maritime rock plants, including the very rare sea lavender *Limonium paradoxum*

ST MARGARET'S ISLAND   Pembroke OS 152 W of Caldy Island, 18 acres. LR managed by West Wales Nats Trust, PVR. A carboniferous limestone islet accessible at very low tide from Caldy, and remarkable chiefly for its sea birds: nesting cormorant, shag, razorbill, guillemot, puffin, great and lesser black-backed, herring and kittiwake gulls, oystercatcher and rock pipit. Grey seals offshore.

SKERRIES   Anglesey OS 106 2 miles off Carmel Head. These scattered low rocks belong to Trinity House, PVR. Nesting sea birds include gulls and terns and some auks; also oystercatcher, rock-pipit, shag and cormorant. Grey seals occasionally pup here, and are always present, basking over low tide.

SKOKHOLM   Pembroke OS 151 off SW of Pembrokeshire, 242 acres. PVR West Wales NT. LR famous for studies carried out at its Bird Observatory, possibly one of the most studied of small islands in the world. Observations began in 1928 by R. M. Lockley (see *The Island*, 1969), and the first British Bird Observatory was opened there in 1933 for the intensive marking of birds. Several thousand now ringed annually, including numbers of small migratory birds, some rarities new to Wales and Britain, each spring and autumn.
Mammals: grey seal, rabbit, house mouse
Birds: breeding pairs—about 35,000 Manx shearwater, 1,000 storm petrels, 800 lesser black-backed and 600 herring gulls (great black-backs are controlled), 550 razorbill, 70 guillemot, 1,500 puffin, 50 oyster-catcher, 27 lapwing, 48 skylark, 30 wheatear, 36 each rock and meadow pipits, 30 starling, 1 or 2 raven, and other species irregularly
Plants: typical maritime sub-oceanic type flora, conditioned by rabbit grazing, but spectacular displays of bluebell, sea campion, vernal squill, scurvy grass, primrose, thrift. Geology: old red sandstone

SKOMER ISLAND   Pembroke OS 151 off SW Pembroke, 722 acres excluding the small islet to the east (Middleholm, 21½ acres PRI). NNR managed by the West Wales NT. Landing fee of 5s to non-members. Boats from nearby mainland at Martinshaven. Permission to stay overnight from WWNT. This very fine NNR has a resident warden, and chalets for visiting members of the WWNT. In many respects it resembles Skokholm, but the rocks are varied and chiefly basaltic (see

Buxton & Lockley, 1950), the cliffs higher and more spectacular, and the fauna more varied.

Mammals: unique vole (*Clethrionomys glareolus skomerensis*), wood mouse common and pygmy shrews. About 50 grey seal pups born in caves and on beaches each autumn

Birds: as for Skokholm, but very few storm petrels, and many more razorbills, guillemots and puffins. About 1,500 pairs of kittiwake nest on sheer cliffs; more pairs of ravens; and there are nesting chough, short-eared owl, buzzard, curlew, cormorant, shag, pheasant, and (less often today) peregrine falcon. There is a good deal of bramble and other low cover in which dunnock, whitethroat, sedge warbler, blackbird, and linnet nest, as well as, normally, wren. This cover makes it less easy to spot small migrants than on barer Skokholm; but both islands have many migrants spring and autumn, and in winter birds flock to the islands in frosty weather, as it rarely freezes or snows there.

Plants: as for Skokholm, but several more species, especially in the ungrazed cliffs

SNOWDON   See under Welsh name, *Y Wyddfa*

SOUTH STACK cliffs   Anglesey OS 106 Holyhead Island. These tall cliffs (now a little disturbed by climbers) are traditionally the summer home of large numbers of ledge-nesting razorbills, guillemots and kittiwakes. Fulmars also breed, and it is usually possible to see grey seals, which occupy caves there in the sea below.

STACK ROCKS   Pembroke OS 151 6 miles SW of Pembroke town. PA only weekends and evenings. Two limestone pillars detached from the cliffs and within a stone's throw of the grassy parking site. From March to July the crowns are covered with breeding guillemots, the sides with razorbills and kittiwakes. On the adjacent cliffs are raven, chough, buzzard and many pairs of fulmar, herring and great black-backed gulls. This whole coast from St Govan's Head (ancient medieval chapel in the cliff) to Linney Head is within the National Park: at present it is an Army vehicle manœuvring range, and closed on most week-days (times of closure in local papers), but the cliff path is well worth walking for its sea-birds, plants and remarkable limestone caves, blow-holes and arches; also remains of cliff forts of the Iron Age and earlier. Plants include the rare sea lavenders and other lime-loving species.

STRUMBLE HEAD   Pembroke OS 138 5 miles NW of Fishguard, within the National Park. A lighthouse on the farthest point. High cliffs cut by small streams and bays. On the south side is the majestic wall, 450 ft sheer, of Pwll Deri, where buzzard, raven, cormorant, fulmar and gulls breed, and below there are caves and pebble beaches where grey seals pup in the autumn. Choughs can be seen here in small flocks.

TALYLLYN   See under Lakes

TOWY VALLEY   See under *Allt Rhyd y Groes, Llyn Brianne Reservoir* and *Gwenffrwd* for details of upper Towy sites (OS 140). Below Llandovery the Towy valley broadens out to form pleasant water meadows with such nesting birds as kingfisher, sand martin, dipper, grey wagtail, sandpiper, and in woods, buzzard, raven, pied flycatcher, redstart and others. In winter up to 1,000 white-fronted geese, typical form, are present in this mid-Towy valley. At Carmarthen (OS 152) the river becomes salt, and the salmon fishermen use their traditional coracles— round boats of lath and canvas skilfully handled with single paddle. There are mile-wide sands and saltings at low tide where the rivers Taf and Gwendraeth mingle with the Towy below Llanstephan; splendid country for wildfowl and wading birds, and many shelduck nest in the sand dunes.

TRAETH BACH   Merioneth OS 116. The broad estuary separating Merioneth and Caernarvon. The dune system of Morfa Harlech extends towards the Caernarvon shore, making a fine inland salt lake, into which the Portmerion peninsula with its wooded shore protrudes. At low tide the estuary is a vast plain of sand traversed by shallow rivers. Near Portmadoc the North Wales Nats' Trust maintain a reserve of 29 acres of dune (PVR NWNT). Much can be seen of the numerous wildfowl and wading bird population autumn to spring, from Portmerion and the toll road A497; but much more from the south side, which is wilder, on foot. Shelduck breed, and the dune flora is rich.

TREGARON BOG   See *Cors Tregaron*

TRAWSFYNYDD LAKE   See under Reservoirs

WHITEFORD   Glamorgan OS 152 NW tip of the Gower peninsula. Nearly 2,000 acres of this large area of sand dune, with some conifer plantation, is a NNR, partly on National Trust land. Includes calcareous dune system, salt-marshes and mudflats. The winter population of wildfowl and waders is noted for its numbers and variety; with small groups of non-breeding arctic species remaining in summer. PVR required from NCSW in the reserved area away from marked paths and the beach. Plants and invertebrates are specially interesting and varied.

WORM'S HEAD   See under Gower

WYNDCLIFF   See under Blackcliff

YNYSHIR   Cardigan OS 127 near Eglwysfach, Machynlleth, about 800 acres. New RSPB reserve. Warden, W. M. Condry. PVR RSPB. Edge of Dovey Estuary (see above). Mixed ecology of saltings, freshwater marsh, peat bog, small rocky hills with sessile oaks, patches of conifers, stream, waterfall, and a disused eighteenth-century iron-smelting mill (scheduled Ancient Monument). Interesting birds include: buzzard, pied flycatcher, redstart, dipper, a heronry, waders and ducks (especially nesting merganser and shelduck).
Mammals: otter and polecat

Y WYDDFA (Snowdon)   OS 107 9 miles south of Bangor. The largest NNR in Wales, 4,145 acres, of which 150 is low-lying oakwood, the rest windswept sheepwalks and moorland rising to the arctic-alpine plant zone at over 3,000 ft. It is part of the Snowdon National Park, with public access, but PVR to visit enclosed parts and to collect specimens. NCNW.

Field Study Centres
The Field Studies Council, 9 Devereux Court, Strand, London, WC2, maintains three Field Centres in Wales, and a fourth in the Welsh Marches near Shrewsbury. Each is open between March and November for the accommodation of field naturalists and other observers and students of outdoor subjects, including artists. While the majority of the sixty or so beds at each centre are booked by parties of sixth-form students, groups and individuals of all ages are welcome, either to join

in the programme of weekly courses (in geology, geography, botany, zoology, ornithology, archaeology, meteorology, painting, etc), or to conduct field studies independently. The accommodation is often booked up months ahead, so early application is advisable, to the Warden at the chosen Centre. Facilities of library and laboratory are excellent.

Membership of the Field Studies Council is open to anyone interested, whether for the purpose of using the Centres, or of supporting the Council's work.

DALE FORT CENTRE, Haverfordwest, Pembrokeshire. Situated within the National Park at Dale Point, the western side of the Milford Haven entrance. A Victorian fort, modernised and converted, with laboratories and salt-water aquaria added. Ideal for littoral and marine studies, including exposed cliff and shallow estuary.

ORIELTON FIELD CENTRE, Pembroke. Gracious manor house on Norman foundation with Regency-style interior. Extensive stables block converted to laboratories, lecture and library facilities. Walled estate with about 100 acres of wood and water. The rugged limestone coast lies close to the south, the sheltered haven of Milford with developing oil port to the north. Close by is Orielton Duck Decoy (see page 194).

PRESTON MONTFORD CENTRE, near Shrewsbury. On a rural estate with access to River Severn and ideal for excursions into the hills of mid-eastern Wales.

RHYD-Y-CRENAU (the Drapers' Field Centre), Betwys-y-Coed, Caerns. Attractive converted mansion from which there is easy access to Snowdonia, mountains, moorland, wooded valleys, as well as the coast of North Wales.

CHAPTER EIGHT

Index of Welsh birds

With notes on distribution

SPECIES ARE PLACED in alphabetical order for ease of reference, not in systematic order which has ever been a matter for disagreement among taxonomists, resulting in changes confusing to the beginner. In our list the family name is given first, then the adjective or specific name, and last the current scientific name. Rarities of which less than half a dozen have been recorded within the present century are omitted; very many of these are reported only at the bird observatories of Skokholm and Bardsey.

AUK Little *Plantus alle* Irregular winter visitor, sometimes blown inland
AVOCET *Recurvirostra avosetta* Rare, chiefly winter
BEE-EATER *Merops apiaster* Very rare, summer
BITTERN *Botaurus stellaris* Irregular, chiefly winter, has bred Anglesey
BLACKBIRD *Turdus merula* Abundant resident and winter visitor, nesting on most of the small islands also
BLACKCAP *Sylvia atricapilla* Common summer, all counties, a few in winter
BRAMBLING *Fringilla montifringilla* Regular winter, small numbers with chaffinches, especially along coast
BULLFINCH *Pyrrhula pyrrhula* Common, woods and gardens, increasing
BUNTING
    CIRL *Emberiza cirlus* Formerly breeding, at present irregular visitor
    CORN *Emberiza calandra* Formerly common resident, today confined to isolated colonies along English border, decreasing

LAPLAND *Calcarius lapponicus* Chiefly late autumn visitor to coastal counties, easily overlooked

ORTOLAN *Emberiza hortulana* Scarce visitor, spring and autumn

REED *Emberiza schoeniclus* Widely distributed resident, breeding some islands

SNOW *Plectrophenax nivalis* Scarce winter visitor, coast and mountain

YELLOW *Emberiza citrinella* Resident, especially common open furze-grown country, and new plantations while trees are small

BUZZARD *Buteo buteo* Characteristic resident in wilder country and sea-cliffs (page 83)

ROUGH-LEGGED *Buteo lagopus* Very rare winter visitor

CHAFFINCH *Fringilla coelebs* Most numerous finch, both as resident and winter visitor. Large flocks pass through in autumn

CHIFFCHAFF *Phylloscopus collybita* Common summer breeder, especially coast woods, less numerous than willow warbler in mountain woods

CHOUGH *Coraxia pyrrhocorax* About 100 pairs distributed western coast counties (page 110)

COOT *Fulica atra* Breeding most large waters and ponds, winter visitor estuaries and reservoirs

CORMORANT *Phalacrocorax carbo* Small nesting colonies along coast. Wandering far inland to fish rivers and lakes, and south to Spain in winter (page 119)

CORNCRAKE See *Rail, Land*

CRAKE

SPOTTED *Porzana porzana* Rarely seen, more often heard calling. Has bred rarely in several counties

LITTLE *Porzana parva* Very rare, chiefly winter

CREEPER

TREE *Certhia familiaris* Common resident wooded areas, wandering to treeless islands in autumn

CROSSBILL *Loxia curvirostra* Scarce, mostly late summer and winter visitor. Has nested sporadically, not yet established as a regular breeder, but may soon, as conifer plantations increase and mature

CROW

CARRION *Corvus corone* Widespread resident, from treeless islands to inland woods, and mountains to 1,500 ft

HOODED *Corvus cornix* Irregular winter visitor

CUCKOO *Cuculus canorus* Common summer visitor, most numerous lowland moors and hills

CURLEW *Numenius arquata* Widespread resident, possibly increasing as a breeder, most numerous on moors up to 1,000 ft. Large flocks on estuaries, some non-breeders spend summer there

DIPPER *Cinclus cinclus* Resident, holding territories all clean mountain streams, and some down to sea-level (page 92)

DIVER

BLACK-THROATED *Colymbus articus* One or two reported at some point on coast each year, chiefly winter

GREAT NORTHERN *Colymbus immer* More regular than black-throated in same situations. Immatures occasionally seen in summer

RED-THROATED *Colymbus stellatus* Most regular of divers on coast in winter, occasionally inland, and immatures in summer

DOTTEREL *Charadrius morinellus* Occasional passage migrant, spring and autumn, chiefly high ground

DOVE

COLLARED *Streptopelia decaocto* New arrival, now resident all counties, especially small towns, suburban areas, farms and villages (page 105)

RING See Woodpigeon

ROCK *Columba livia* Resident on coast. Present flocks are heavily diluted with feral pigeon stock (page 123)

STOCK *Columba oenas* Widely distributed resident, especially well-timbered open country, also sea cliffs

TURTLE *Streptopelia turtur* Summer passage migrant all counties, but breeding regularly only border counties Denbigh to Glamorgan, and most numerous Monmouth

DUCK (see also under *Goosander, Merganser, Shelduck, Smew*)

EIDER *Somateria mollissima* Regular winter visitor to sandy estuaries, especially Dovey, Burry and Anglesey

GADWALL *Anas strepera* Irregular but increasing visitor (also some escapes from wildfowl collections)

GARGANEY *Anas querquedula* Irregular chiefly summer visitor, has bred rarely Anglesey

GOLDENEYE *Bucephala clangula* Regular in small numbers, winter

LONG-TAILED *Clangula hyemalis* Irregular and scarce, winter

MALLARD *Anas platyrhynchos* Abundant nesting and winter visitor

PINTAIL *Anas acuta* Regular winter, occasionally large flocks

POCHARD *Aythya ferina* Common winter visitor, breeding regularly only Anglesey, rarely elsewhere

SCAUP *Aythya marila* Regular, often scarce, winter visitor

SCOTER *Melanitta nigra* Flocks are common offshore in winter, and non-breeding rafts may summer at sea

VELVET SCOTER *Melanitta fusca* Rare but few seen most winters, often in company of last

SHOVELER *Spatula clypeata* Chiefly winter visitor, often large flocks. Breeds regularly Anglesey, sporadically elsewhere

TEAL *Anas crecca* Numerous in winter. Breeds most counties, and high up on mountain pools (page 96)

TUFTED *Aythya fuligula* Common in winter most large sheets of fresh water, and a few pairs remain to breed in some counties

WIGEON *Anas penelope* Abundant winter, estuaries and larger lakes and ponds

DUNLIN *Calidris alpina* Abundant autumn to spring, chiefly along shore, but frequently to inland waters. Breeds sparingly in mountains (page 95)

DUNNOCK *Prunella modularis* Numerous resident, including some small islands

FALCON

PEREGRINE *Falco peregrinus* Over 200 eyries on coast and inland 1930, but now reduced to few pairs (page 86)

FIELDFARE *Turdus pilaris* Common in flocks winter, first arrivals September, lingers until May in uplands

FIRECREST *Regulus ignicapillus* Irregular autumn visitor, but recorded every year in one or other (chiefly coastal) county

FLYCATCHER

PIED *Muscicapa hypoleuca* Passage migrant and summer visitor, breeding all counties save Anglesey, scarce Glamorgan and Pembroke

SPOTTED *Muscicapa striata* Passage migrant and breeding all counties, arriving late (May) and departing September

GANNET *Sula bassana* Seen offshore all coasts. The famous colony at Grassholm estimated at over 15,000 nests (page 186)

GODWIT

BAR-TAILED *Limosa lapponica* Common autumn to spring, chiefly estuaries

BLACK-TAILED *Limosa limosa* Scarce, chiefly estuaries in autumn, occasionally inland, and in spring

GOLDCREST *Regulus regulus* Widely dispersed resident, regularly seen on passage by bird observatories

GOLDFINCH *Carduelis carduelis* Formerly scarce, now common and breeding all counties

GOOSANDER *Mergus merganser* Scarce winter visitor, chiefly border counties

GOOSE

BARNACLE *Branta leucopsis* Rare vagrant visitor, winter; some years no records

BEAN *Anser arvensis* As for barnacle goose, chiefly odd birds shot in winter

BRENT *Branta bernicla* Regular winter visitor to Burry Estuary, a small flock. Rare elsewhere

CANADA *Branta canadensis* Introduced, breeding Anglesey, Montgomery, Pembroke, spreading elsewhere

GREY LAG *Anser anser* Normally a rare winter visitor. Now established ferally from stock introduced Anglesey

PINK-FOOTED *Anser brachyrhynchus* Scarce winter visitor, but may be overlooked associating with next species, eg Dovey Estuary

WHITE-FRONTED *Anser albifrons* Commonest goose visiting Wales, flying to traditional wintering sites Cardigan, Montgomery, Towy valley, lower Severn. Birds of the Greenland race *flavirostris* seem to concentrate at Cors Tregaron, up to 600 maximum in a flock

GREBE

BLACK-NECKED *Podiceps nigricollis* Regular winter visitor small numbers Anglesey (where has bred), Glamorgan, rare elsewhere

GREAT CRESTED *Podiceps cristatus* Breeds sparingly most suitable lakes and large ponds except Glamorgan and Pembroke. Widely distributed in winter

LITTLE *Podiceps ruficollis* Thinly distributed as breeder, but much overlooked. Widespread in winter

RED-NECKED *Podiceps griseigena* Scarce winter vagrant, recorded somewhere in Wales most years, usually singly

SLAVONIAN *Podiceps auritus* Rather more often seen in winter than last species

GREENFINCH *Chloris chloris* Breeding universally. Flocks concentrate on farms and the shore in winter

GREENSHANK *Tringa nebularia* Common in small numbers autumn and spring, a few in winter

GROUSE

BLACK *Lyrurus tetrix* Formerly very scarce, now increasing with increased plantation cover (page 97)

RED *Lagopus scoticus* Thinly distributed heather moorland

GUILLEMOT

BLACK *Uria grylle* Stray summer visitor to western coasts. Has bred Great Orme and Anglesey

COMMON *Uria aalge* Breeding steep cliffs Anglesey, Caernarvon, Cardigan, Pembroke, Gower. Numbers declining (page 116). Widespread in winter

GULL

BLACK-HEADED *Larus ridibundus* Resident, increasing, breeding most counties. Abundant winter (page 97)

COMMON *Larus canus* Widespread winter visitor in moderate numbers

GLAUCOUS *Larus hyperboreus* Rare vagrant

GREAT BLACK-BACKED *Larus marinus* Resident, breeding all rocky coasts (page 113)

HERRING *Larus argentatus* The most numerous resident gull, but does not breed flat shores of Flint, Carmarthen. Large flocks far inland in winter

KITTIWAKE *Rissa tridactyla* Breeding steep cliffs all coasts save Merioneth, Carmarthen, Monmouth and Flint (page 114)

LESSER BLACK-BACKED *Larus fuscus* Summer visitor, arriving February–March. Has bred inland but main colonies along coast, largest Anglesey, Pembs islands, Flatholm (page 113)

HARRIER

HEN *Circus cyaneus* Scarce winter visitor to moorland and open country. Some remain late, and occasionally breed

MARSH *Circus aeruginosus* Rare, chiefly spring and autumn, but has attempted to breed Anglesey

MONTAGU'S *Circus pygargus* Summer visitor, often seen on migration. Has bred several counties, now rarely nesting

HAWFINCH *Coccothraustes coccothraustes* Rare vagrant most counties, but breeds in very small numbers in south-east

HAWK

SPARROW *Accipiter nisus* Breeding all counties, no observable decrease

HERON *Ardea cinerea* Nesting all counties except Flint and Denbigh, wandering widely July to end of year (page 100)

HOBBY *Falco subbuteo* Chiefly rare summer vagrant, but has bred south-east irregularly

HOOPOE *Upupa epops* Regular but erratic and scarce visitor on spring and autumn migration, usually singles

JACKDAW *Corvus monedula* Numerous resident

JAY *Garrulus glandarius* Widespread resident all woodlands

KESTREL *Falco tinnunculus* Common resident

KINGFISHER *Alcedo atthis* Resident in small numbers clear streams, rivers, lakes, canals, wandering much July to February, visiting coasts

KITE *Milvus milvus* About twenty pairs surviving mid-Wales, the only British colony (page 81)

KNOT *Calidris canutus* Winter visitor, chiefly large estuaries, a few non-breeders remain all summer

LAPWING *Vanellus vanellus* Breeds all counties and some small islands. Often large flocks in winter

LARK

SHORE *Eremophila alpestris* Rare visitor cold months

SKY *Alauda arvensis* Numerous resident, nesting from sea-level to mountain top

WOOD *Lullula arborea* Formerly common, especially upland farms. Now scarce but slowly recovering from severe winter of 1963 (page 110)

LINNET *Carduelis cannabina* Common resident, especially coast. Numbers migrate south over winter

MAGPIE *Pica pica* Common resident, nesting occasionally small islands

MALLARD See under *Duck*

MARTIN

HOUSE *Delichon urbica* Summer breeder widespread, including cliff-nesting colonies

SAND *Riparia riparia* Widespread summer breeder, less numerous in west

MERGANSER

RED-BREASTED *Mergus serrator* Regular but scarce winter visitor. Has lately bred Anglesey, Dovey estuary, possibly Glamorgan

N

MERLIN *Falco columbarius* Nests sparsely remote moorland, dune and coast. Wandering widely in winter (page 88)

MOORHEN *Gallinula chloropus* Resident beside all waters, from small ponds to large lakes and rivers, and on most offshore islands

NIGHTINGALE *Luscinia megarhynchos* Nesting Monmouth and sparsely east Glamorgan, rare visitor elsewhere

NIGHTJAR *Caprimulgus europaeus* Summer visitor, formerly nesting all counties (page 109), now much rarer but nesting sparsely southern counties

NUTHATCH *Sitta europaea* Greatly increased from 1920 onwards, now common resident all counties, but scarce Anglesey

ORIOLE Golden *Oriolus oriolus* Vagrant, a few individuals recorded every spring and rarely autumn, especially bird observatories

OSPREY *Pandion haliaëtus* Rare visitor, chiefly autumn, seen rather more often since breeding re-established Scotland

OUZEL Ring *Turdus torquatus* Widespread locally on migration. Summer breeder upper valleys and dingles in mountains, not Anglesey, and rarely nesting Pembroke

OWL

BARN *Tyto alba* Widely but thinly spread as resident, numbers fluctuate according to severity of winter

LITTLE *Athene noctua* Introduced earlier in England, first appeared Glamorgan and Monmouth about 1914. Reached Pembroke 1920, Caernarvon 1930. Numerous all counties by 1950; now less common, and inhabiting chiefly open country, especially Anglesey, Glamorgan and Monmouth

LONG-EARED *Asio otus* Very scarce local resident, chiefly conifer woods Cardigan, Brecon, Radnor

SHORT-EARED *Asio flammeus* Scarce resident and winter visitor, a few nesting where voles abound, including new plantations, and regularly Skomer Island

TAWNY *Strix aluco* Widespread, commonest owl, resident from town park to mountain dingle and isolated copse in sea-creek

OYSTERCATCHER *Haematopus ostralegus* Resident all coasts save Monmouth. Large concentrations on island sanctuaries and cockle beds (page 120)

PARTRIDGE *Perdix perdix* Has become scarce in most counties, probably due to decline of gamekeeping and increase of pesticides on land. Survives chiefly in corn and root-growing districts

RED-LEGGED *Alectoris rufa* Introduced and re-introduced, but does not seem to survive for long if unprotected, save perhaps North Wales

PETREL

FULMAR *Fulmarus glacialis* As a breeder still spreading all coasts, but not yet nesting flat shores of Flint, Merioneth, Carmarthen, Monmouth (page 118)

LEACH'S *Oceanodroma leucorrhoa* Occasional autumn and winter visitor, often found dead on shore after gales

STORM *Hydrobates pelagicus* Main colony at least 1,000 pairs Skokholm, a few pairs Skomer, Bardsey, and possibly other smaller islets. Seen offshore by day, especially Bristol Channel (page 118)

PHALAROPE

GREY *Phalaropus fulicarius* Irregular visitor, chiefly autumn, some winter, to coast and inland waters

RED-NECKED *Phalaropus lobatus* Very rare autumn passage migrant

PHEASANT *Phasianus colchicus* Introduced and surviving ferally all counties (even where not raised artificially). Has survived ferally for fifty years on Skomer

PIGEON See *Woodpigeon*

PIPIT

MEADOW *Anthus pratensis* Characteristic summer breeder open wilder country, from grassy island and shore dune to mountains above tree-line. Some winter on lower ground, many fly south in autumn, and there is a passage migration of northern breeding birds

TREE *Anthus trivialis* Widespread summer visitor, nesting upland fields with trees, plantations, less common along coast and absent Anglesey except on migration

ROCK *Anthus spinoletta petrosus* Resident all rocky shores, wandering in winter. The European mountain (water) pipit *A. s. spinoletta* is a subspecies occasionally identified in Wales in winter

PLOVER

GOLDEN *Charadrius apricarius* Limited breeder on high ground (page 95), perhaps declining due to afforestation of habitat. Common winter visitor, numbers erratic, often many hundreds coast and lowlands

GREY   *Charadrius squatarola*   Regular visitor small numbers August to May. Up to 700 have been counted Monmouth coast

KENTISH   *Charadrius alexandrinus*   Very rare migrant, summer

LITTLE RINGED   *Charadrius dubius*   Occasional summer, not breeding

RINGED   *Charadrius hiaticula*   Breeding suitable pebble/sandy beaches, occasionally rocky cliffs. Numerous in winter

PUFFIN   *Fratercula arctica*   Main nesting concentrations Skomer and Skokholm, few colonies now left on mainland cliffs and islets elsewhere in Anglesey, Caernarvon and Pembroke. Decreasing (page 115)

QUAIL   *Coturnix coturnix*   Erratic summer visitor, odd pairs have bred most counties, almost regularly Monmouth

RAIL

LAND   *Crex crex*   A once numerous breeder, its loud rasping note familiar all counties. Decrease since 1916 coincides with the earlier hay harvest with machinery. Remained common for another twenty years in upland region of late harvest. Now virtually disappeared as a breeding bird, although occasionally heard in spring, and a few regularly seen on migration at bird observatories

WATER   *Rallus aquaticus*   Passage migrant, frequently killed at lighthouses, and winter resident, especially to frost-free coast and islands. Very few pairs remain to breed, probably more than is supposed, due to skulking habits. Has bred Skokholm

RAVEN   *Corvus corax*   More ravens breed in Wales than elsewhere in the British Isles (per 10 mile square). Tree nests frequent in areas lacking cliffs (page 85)

RAZORBILL   *Alca torda*   Breeds coasts Anglesey, Caernarvon, Cardigan, Pembroke and Gower. Largest numbers Skomer, Skokholm, Ramsey

REDPOLL   *Carduelis flammea*   Breeding commonly in upland plantations, erratic elsewhere but increasing. Wanders in small flocks, often with siskins, in winter

REDSHANK   *Tringa totanus*   Common and widely distributed all shores and frequently inland in winter. A few pairs nest all counties, especially wet moors and upland bogs

SPOTTED   *Tringa erythropus*   Erratic winter visitor, also seen most counties in summer although not breeding

REDSTART   *Phoenicurus phoenicurus*   Summer breeder areas well provided with trees. Absent Anglesey and coasts of south

BLACK *Phoenicurus ochruros* Regular but erratic spring visitor, less common than 1940–50 decade. A few in autumn and winter, chiefly south-west coast

REDWING *Turdus musicus* Regular on passage and many remain to winter, large numbers retreat to mild coast in hard weather. Occasionally lingers into May

ROBIN *Erithacus rubecula* Very common resident and passage migrant. Takes up winter territory on small islands, and sometimes stays to breed there

ROOK *Corvus frugilegus* Numerous resident, rookeries all counties, up to at least 800 ft above sea level

RUFF *Philomachus pugnax* Passage migrant small numbers chiefly autumn, a few in spring

SANDERLING *Crocethia alba* Passage migrant autumn to spring, not abundant

SANDPIPER

COMMON *Tringa hypoleucos* Summer visitor, nesting by clear upland pools and streams. Widespread on migration, often solitary, sometimes in winter

CURLEW *Calidris testacea* Scarce on passage, chiefly September–November

GREEN *Tringa ochropus* Regular but scarce on passage inland marsh, stream and fresh water, chiefly July–October

PURPLE *Calidris maritima* Common on rocky shores September–May, a few non-breeders remain all summer

WOOD *Tringa glareola* Rare autumn vagrant

SCOTER See under *Duck*

SHAG *Phalacrocorax aristotelis* Resident, breeding small numbers all rocky coasts

SHEARWATER

GREAT *Procellaria gravis* Rare offshore, but increasing observation may establish this and the similar-sized Cory's shearwater *P. diomedea* as fairly regular in autumn with Sooty and Manx species, as they are along the south coast of Ireland

SOOTY *Procellaria grisea* Sea-watches have established that this shearwater passes offshore western Wales regularly in autumn

MANX *Procellaria puffinus* Probably over 35,000 pairs nest at Skokholm, and as many or more at Skomer. About 2–3,000 pairs Bardsey. Eggs occasionally reported in burrows on mainland cliffs elsewhere on west coast (page 117). The Balearic race *P. p. mauretanicus* reported most autumns off west coast

SHELDUCK   *Tadorna tadorna*   Breeding small numbers almost all extensive sandy shores and muddy estuaries. Many nests placed some miles inland. Adults migrate July to North Sea (page 121–2), returning after moult by December

SHRIKE

GREAT GREY   *Lanius excubitor*   Vagrant, singles generally recorded most winter months each year

LESSER GREY   *Lanius minor*   Very rare vagrant, summer

RED-BACKED SHRIKE   *Lanius collurio*   Formerly widespread as summer breeder, now largely a scarce passage migrant, nesting only sporadically in south-east

WOODCHAT   *Lanius senator*   Recorded in most summers as stray migrant

SISKIN   *Carduelis spinus*   A few pairs nest in central counties, otherwise seen sparingly most counties autumn to spring

SKUA

ARCTIC   *Stercorarius parasiticus*   Regular on passage offshore in autumn, more rarely in spring

GREAT   *Stercorarius skua*   Less common than last on passage

LONG-TAILED   *Stercorarius longicaudus*   Scarce on passage, a few most years

POMARINE   *Stercorarius pomarinus*   As for last species

SKYLARK   See under *Lark*

SMEW   *Mergus albellus*   Very scarce visitor, a few recorded each winter

SNIPE

COMMON   *Capella gallinago*   Breeding sparsely all counties, more numerous winter

GREAT   *Capella media*   Very rare passage migrant autumn, a few spring

JACK   *Lymnocryptes minimus*   Winter visitor all counties

SPARROW

HEDGE   See *Dunnock*

HOUSE   *Passer domesticus*   Abundant resident except locally in some isolated western parishes

TREE   *Passer montanus*   Chiefly scarce winter visitor to western counties, but breeding Anglesey and eastern counties

SPOONBILL *Platalea leucorodia* Rare visitor to south, chiefly summer

STARLING *Sturnus vulgaris* Common resident, rare as breeder in a few isolated western parishes. Huge influx in winter

ROSE-COLOURED *Sturnus roseus* Very rare vagrant

STINT Little *Calidris minuta* Scarce but regular passage migrant, autumn and winter

STONECHAT *Saxicola torquata* Resident all coast counties where there is extensive gorse cover. Many died in severe winter of 1963, since when fewer pairs now breed inland counties

SWALLOW *Hirundo rustica* Common summer visitor, nesting from small islands to mountain farms

SWAN
BEWICK'S *Cygnus bewickii* Regular winter visitor most counties
MUTE *Cygnus olor* Common resident. Large flocks of non-breeders on some estuaries
WHOOPER *Cygnus cygnus* Regular winter visitor in small parties

SWIFT *Apus apus* Common summer visitor, breeding most towns and villages but rare or scarce as nester in some western sea-coast villages

TEAL See under *Duck*

TERN
ARCTIC *Sterna macrura* Summer visitor, definitely breeding only Anglesey, Caernarvon and Flint
BLACK *Chlidonias niger* Scarce on passage spring and autumn
COMMON *Sterna hirundo* Same breeding distribution as Arctic, with which it is often confused; cautious observers may refer to 'Comic' (Common/Arctic) terns, especially where both are seen on migration offshore or over inland waters
LITTLE *Sterna albifrons* Summer visitor, nesting less freely as its sandy breeding ground is invaded by caravans, etc. Now nests only northern coast counties Merioneth to Flint (page 115)
ROSEATE *Sterna dougallii* Scarce summer visitor, breeding only Anglesey
SANDWICH *Sterna sandvicensis* Recorded most counties as passage migrant in small numbers. A few pairs occasionally breed Anglesey

THRUSH
MISTLE *Turdus viscivorus* Resident all districts with trees
SONG *Turdus ericetorum* More numerous than last, but less so than

blackbird. Nests also in more open country, migrating to low ground for winter

TIT

BLUE *Parus caeruleus* Most numerous resident tit, visits small islands and treeless coasts in winter

COAL *Parus ater* Widespread but local resident all counties

GREAT *Parus major* Numerous resident

LONG-TAILED *Aegithalos caudatus* Common resident, even in some isolated coastal woods, but rather scarce Anglesey

MARSH *Parus palustris* Common resident all counties except Anglesey, Caernarvon and Merioneth, where rare

WILLOW *Parus atricapillus* Frequently mistaken for Marsh Tit and less often recorded. Evidently thinly distributed and breeding all counties except Anglesey, but distribution still requires working out (page 109)

TREE CREEPER *Certhia familiaris* Common resident all woodlands and well-timbered country

TURNSTONE *Arenaria interpres* Winter visitor, resident all coasts September–April, small numbers non-breeders spend summer on rocky coasts

TWITE *Carduelis flavirostris* Only a vagrant to most of Wales, except north-east, where small numbers winter and some nest, chiefly along border with Cheshire

WAGTAIL

GREY *Motacilla cinerea* Resident most fast-running unpolluted streams, wandering in winter

PIED *Motacilla alba yarelli* Resident, nesting even on small islands

WHITE *Motacilla a. alba* This subspecies appears on migration, often with *yarelli*, March–May and September–October

YELLOW *Motacilla flava* Summer visitor, nesting regularly all border counties, rarely farther west, where it is chiefly seen on passage

WARBLER

BARRED *Sylvia nisoria* Rare vagrant, chiefly autumn at bird observatories

GARDEN *Sylvia borin* Summer visitor, nesting all counties in tangled woodlands, thickets, young plantations, most frequent sheltered inland valleys

GRASSHOPPER *Locustella naevia* Summer visitor, nesting commons, low coverts, gorse, boggy vegetation

MELODIOUS *Hippolais polyglotta* Rare on passage summer, chiefly bird observatories

REED *Acrocephalus scirpaceus* Summer visitor, nesting eastern border counties including Glamorgan, rarely elsewhere

SEDGE *Acrocephalus schoenobaenus* Numerous passage migrant and summer nester, often on remote islands

WILLOW *Phylloscopus trochilus* Abundant on passage and nesting

WOOD *Phylloscopus sibilatrix* Summer visitor, nesting chiefly old deciduous woodland. Scarce on coast, does not breed Anglesey

YELLOW-BROWED *Phylloscopus inornatus* Rare vagrant, chiefly recorded bird observatories

WAXWING *Bombycilla garrulus* Irregular winter visitor, occasionally small flocks

WHEATEAR *Oenanthe oenanthe* Summer visitor and passage migrant, nesting bare cliffs, mountain screes, dry-walled treeless uplands. Most numerous on offshore islands (Skokholm about forty pairs). The Greenland race *O. o. leucorrhoa* passes through Wales both spring and autumn

WHIMBREL *Numenius arquata* Regular passage migrant late-April–mid-May and autumn. A very few may overwinter

WHINCHAT *Saxicola rubetra* Summer visitor, nesting all counties, chiefly upland districts. Scarce Anglesey and lowland of Pembroke, Glamorgan, Monmouth

WHITETHROAT *Sylvia communis* Numerous summer visitor, nesting even on small islands, and abundant passage migrant

LESSER *Sylvia curruca* Summer visitor, nesting regularly eastern counties, irregularly elsewhere. Scarce on migration west coast

WIGEON See under *Duck*

WOODCOCK *Scolopax rusticola* Common winter visitor, in hard weather large numbers retreat to coast and islands. Nests rather sporadically but easily overlooked in damp woods through nocturnal habits

WOODPECKER

GREAT SPOTTED *Dendrocopus major* Widespread resident in suitable timbered country, scarcer along west coast and Anglesey

GREEN *Picus viridis* Widespread resident. Numbers fluctuate

LESSER SPOTTED *Dendrocopus minor* Not often seen, but nesting sparsely all counties, especially along border

WOODPIGEON *Columba palumbus* Numerous resident, nesting from high mountain plantations to scrub on sea cliffs. Large flocks in winter

WREN *Troglodytes troglodytes* Abundant resident. Some winter on small islands where they do not nest (Skokholm, Grassholm)

WRYNECK *Jynx torquilla* An increasingly rare passage migrant, chiefly recorded singly at Skokholm and Bardsey. (Formerly bred Glamorgan and Monmouth)

YELLOWHAMMER See under *Bunting, Yellow*

Bibliography

Bardsey Bird & Field Observatory Reports, 1953–69
Benoit, P. and Richards, M. *A contribution to the flora of Merioneth* (W Wales Nats Trust, Haverfordwest, 1963)
Berry, R. J. *The Skokholm mouse; chance and change.* Skokholm BO Report 1967 (W Wales Nats Trust, 1967)
Bolam, George. *Wild life in Wales* (1913)
Borrow, George. *Wild Wales* (1851)
Buxton, J. and Lockley, R. M. *Island of Skomer* (1950)
Cardiff Naturalists' Society. *Transactions.* 1900–69
Clapham, A. R., Tutin, T. G. and Warburg, E. F. *Flora of the British Isles* (Cambridge, 1962)
Condry, W. M. *The Snowdonia National Park* (1967)
Crowcroft, P. *The life of the shrew* (1957)
Findlay, W. P. K. *Wayside and woodland fungi* (1967)
Giraldus Cambrensis (12th century). *The itinerary through Wales The description of Wales*, trans from Latin
Goodier, R. 'Welsh mountain spiders', *Nature in Wales*, 10 (1967), pp 106–14
'Welsh mountain beetles', *Nature in Wales*, 11 (1968), pp 57–67
Hamilton, S. *The flora of Monmouthshire* (Newport, Mon, 1909)
Holyoak, D. T. and Ratcliffe, D. A. 'Distribution of the raven in Britain and Ireland', *Bird Study*, 15 (1968), pp 191–7
Hurrell, H. G. *Wildlife tame but free* (Newton Abbot, 1968)
Hyde, H. A. *Welsh timber trees* (National Museum of Wales, Cardiff, 1962)
Hyde, H. A. and Wade, A. E. *Welsh flowering plants* (Nat Mus Wales, 1957)
Welsh ferns (Nat Mus Wales, 1962)

Lockley, R. M. *The private life of the rabbit* (1964)
  Grey seal, common seal (1966)
  The island (1969)
May, R. F. *A list of the flowering plants and ferns of Carmarthenshire* (W Wales Nats Trust, Haverfordwest, 1967)
McMillan, N. F. *British shells* (1968)
Milner, C., Goodier, R. and Crook, I. G. 'Feral goats in Wales', *Nature in Wales*, 11 (1968), pp 3–11
National Parks Guides (HMSO)
Naturalists' Trusts in Wales. Reports and Bulletins
Nature Conservancy Reports for Wales
Nature in Wales, 1955–69
Nicholson, E. M. *Britain's nature reserves* (1957)
North, F. J. *The river scenery at the head of the Vale of Neath* (Nat Mus Wales, 1962)
Oakley, K. P. 'The date of the Red Lady of Paviland', *Antiquity*, 42 (1968), pp 306–7
Phillips, O. *Gower* (1956)
Riddelsdell, H. J. 'A flora of Glamorganshire', *Journ Botany*, 45 (1907), supplement
Roberts, E. and Roberts, R. H. 'Plant notes from south-east Caernarvonshire', *Proc Bot Soc Br Isles*, 5 (1963), pp 106–16
Rogers, A. E. F. and Gault, L. N. 'Distribution of sand-martins on the river Usk', *Nature in Wales*, 11 (1968), pp 15–19
Rowlands, I. W. 'Reproduction of the Skomer vole', *Nature in Wales*, 11 (1969), pp 169–75
Shorten, M. *Squirrels* (1954)
Skokholm Bird Observatory Reports, 1933–69
Trow, A. H. *The flora of Glamorgan* (Cardiff, 1911)
Wells, A. K. *Outline of historical geology* (1937)
Witherby, H. F. *et al. The Handbook of British Birds* (1952)

Useful addresses

Field Studies Council Centres, see page 201
National Library of Wales, Aberystwyth
National Museum of Wales, Cardiff
National Parks
  Brecon Beacons: the Clerk, County Hall, Brecon
  Pembrokeshire Coast: the Clerk, County Offices, Haverford-
    west
  Snowdonia: the Clerk, County Offices, Penarlag, Dolgellau
National Trust, Napier House, Spilman Street, Carmarthen
Naturalists' Trusts
  Brecknock County: the Hon General Secretary, H. M. Budgen,
    Y Byddwn, Llanhamlach, Brecon
  Glamorgan County: Hon Secretary, address care of the National
    Museum of Wales, Cardiff
  Monmouth: Hon Secretary, 40 Melbourne Way, Newport,
    Mon
  North Wales: Hon Secretary, Dr W. S. Lacey, Dept Botany,
    University College, Bangor, Caerns
  Radnor (Hereford & Radnor Nature Trust): care of the Secre-
    tary, Community Council, County Offices, Llandrindod
    Wells
  West Wales: care of the Secretary, Community Council,
    4 Victoria Place, Haverfordwest, Pem
Nature Conservancy
  North Wales: Penrhos Road, Bangor, Caerns
  South Wales: Plas Gogerddan, Aberystwyth, Cards

Royal Society for the Protection of Birds
  Particulars of Reserves from main office: The Lodge, Sandy, Beds
South Wales Caving Club: 1-10 Powell Street, Penwyllt, Ystradgynlas, S Wales
Youth Hostels: Regional Office, 35 Park Place, Cardiff

Acknowledgments

ALTHOUGH THE WRITING of this book has been my own enter-
prise and responsibility, my best thanks are due to the many
fellow naturalists who have helped in various ways, especially
those who have contributed to *Nature in Wales*. As one of the
founders and editors of this journal of the naturalists' trusts in
Wales, I have had access to, and made full use of, the published
records and articles in rounding off my own field observations
for this book.

In particular I would express my sincere appreciation of the
work of Peter Benoit, William Condry, T. A. W. Davis, P. E.
Davis, J. W. Donovan, J. O. Evans, P. Hope Jones, W. S. Lacey,
Dillwyn Miles, P. M. Miles, Joan Morgan, P. J. Panting, W. S.
Peach, B. L. Sage, D. R. Saunders, H. R. H. and I. M. Vaughan,
L. S. V. Venables and the several authors named in the biblio-
graphy. D. W. Ovenden drew most of the figures.

For courtesy, advice and use of records I acknowledge with
pleasure the assistance of the staffs of the National Museum of
Wales, of the Nature Conservancy's Welsh offices, and of the
Bird Observatories of Skokholm and Bardsey. My old friend
Charles Tunnicliffe, RA, whose beautiful drawings have appeared on successive covers of *Nature in Wales*, has allowed me
to reproduce two here—most fittingly.

R. M. L.

General Index

Most of the scientific names of mentioned species are given under their appropriate chapters, and can be found by looking up the page numbers against the English names below. Bird species not listed below will be found in the alphabetical index of birds, pages 203–18. Italic figures indicate illustrations.